THE • KITCHEN
CASANOVA

*A Gentleman's Guide To Gourmet
Entertaining For Two*

D. L. WILSON

A Shapolsky Book

For any additional information, contact:
Shapolsky Publishers, Inc.
136 W. 22nd Street
New York, NY 10011
212 / 633-2022

First Edition 1990

1 2 3 4 5 6 7 8 9 10

Library of Congress Cataloging-in-Publication Data

Wilson, D.L.
The Kitchen Casanova: a gentleman's guide to gourmet entertaining
for two/D.L. Wilson.
    p. cm.
Reprint, Originally published: Yardley, Pa, Yardley Press, c 1984.
ISBN 0-944007-88-0; $18.95
1. Cookery for two. 2. Menus, 3. Entertaining, I. Title.
TX652.W56 1990
641.5'61--dc20   90-8197
                                                      CIP

ISBN: 0-944007-88-0

Cover Photograph: Georg Klenovsky, Vienna, Austria
Cover Models: Helga Scheidl
              Christian Eder
Design: Anthony Frizano
Menu Photographs: Alfred Paul
Typography: Smith, Inc., NY, NY

A special thanks to the many friends and relatives who tested the menus.

To Michele:

Who made the research for "The Kitchen Casanova" challenging, pleasurable and, above all, conclude with a happy ending to last a lifetime.

Contents

Introduction

This book is designed for all of us who don't know fricassees from cassoulets. In our fast moving society the single man would many times prefer the intimacy and relaxed atmosphere of his home or apartment for entertaining a date. The primary deterent is his lack of confidence in being able to prepare and present a tasty and exciting dining experience. With this book as a guide, anyone can prepare meals that will guarantee to bring a date back for an encore performance.

Enclosed herein are the long held secrets of a kitchen ''klutz'' who traded his French cookbooks for some common sense and succeeded.

The usual cookbook describes, too often in technical terms, how to prepare meat, fish, poultry, vegetables, sauces, appetizers and desserts. For the average novice a great problem is encountered in deciding which appetizer goes with which entree, goes with which vegetable, goes with which dessert. If this stumbling block is surmounted then how do you get everything to come out at the right times? All recipes in this book are presented as part of a complete menu with chronological instructions in preparing the total meal so you won't be serving dessert before the entree.

The method of preparation of all menus in this book follows a set pattern. With a few trial runs and understanding guests, this pattern can be easily mastered and you will be ready to become the maestro of the kitchen.

Along with the step by step instructions on preparing a meal and shopping for the ingredients, there are guides for setting up the basic Kitchen Casanova kitchen, using the kitchen, instructions on setting the table, a guide to wine selection, the art of presentation of a meal and Après Dining techniques.

Simplicity is the catch word of this book. Cooking does not have to be complicated to be good and entertaining. As you will realize after reading the text, a little flair and proper preparation are the key to becoming a successful Kitchen Casanova.

Preparing The Kitchen

"**A** workman is only as good as his tools", is a phrase with which we are all familiar. In order to perform well in the kitchen a cook should have good tools. This does not necessarily mean the most expensive set of imported cookwear or a fancy food processor. The following section will outline setting up the Kitchen Casanova kitchen listing the Basic Necessities for preparing the meals set forth in this book and Useful Additions to either make your work easier or enhance meal presentation. The list is not comprehensive but is a good beginning.

A good rule of thumb is to purchase the best equipment you can afford since cheap tools wear out quickly and many times may not perform satisfactorily. Since we never outgrow the necessity to eat, a well equipped quality kitchen can be enjoyed for a lifetime.

BASIC NECESSITIES

Meal Preparation

Can Opener
  Electric or manual.
Cork Screw
Cutting Board
  Hardwood is preferable to plastic.
Grater
Knives
  Paring knife and 8'' chef's knife. Carbon steel is best but stainless steel is easier to care for. All carbon steel knives should be rinsed and dried immediately after use to prevent corrosion.
Large Serving Spoons
  Three are needed with one being slotted.
Measuring Cups
  U.S. Standard.
Measuring Spoons
  U.S. Standard.

Pot Holders
  At least two.
Serving Bowls
  Three are needed.
Sharpening Steel
  Necessary to keep your knives finely honed and ready to slice, chop, dice or julienne.
Vegetable Peeler

Cooking

Casseroles
  Two with tight fitting lids.
Coffee Pot
  Percolator or instant.
Fry Pan
  10'' size made of heavy guage material is best since it diffuses heat well and eliminates hot spots. It should include a tight fitting lid.

Pie Tin or Glass Pie Dish
8'' diameter.
Sauce Pans
A 1 quart and a 3 quart size, each with tight fitting lid.
Tea Kettle
Vegetable Steamer

Table
Dishes
Should include dinner plate, salad plate, vegetable or dessert dish, cup and saucer. China is best but Ironstone is made in many attractive patterns and can take more abuse and withstand moderate heat.

Flatware
Stainless, Silverplate or Silver.
Water Glasses or Goblets
Wine Glasses
6 to 9 oz. all purpose glasses will suffice. The thinner the glass, the better. Red wine glasses should have larger bowls than white wine glasses.

Accessories
Dish Cloths
Dish Detergent
Dish Towels
Scouring Pads

USEFUL ADDITIONS

Meal Preparation
Bottle Opener
Cannisters
Flour, sugar and pasta.
Colander
Egg Beater or Mixer
Hand or electric.
Garlic Press
Juicer
Knives
6'' chef's knife, boning knife, meat slicer, bread knife, and fruit/vegetable knife.
Ladles
Meat Fork
Mixing Bowls
Three are needed.
Pastry Brush
Plexiglass Cookbook Holder
Salad Bowls
Serving Platter
Soup Crocks
Spatula
Tenderizing Mallet
Tongs
Vegetable Keepers
Vegetable Scrub Brush
Vegetable Spinner

Cooking

Baster
Bulb type.
Chafing Dish
Meat Thermometer
Omelet Pan
Skewers
Timer

Table
Bread Basket
Candlesticks and Candles
Floral Table Centerpiece
Large Goblets, Sherbet Glasses and Snifters
Linen Napkins and Napkin Rings
Linen Table Cloth
Steak Knives
Wine Carafe

Accessories
Apron
Aluminum Foil
Containers for Leftovers
Dust Pan and Brush
Freezer Wrap
Garbage Can with Lid
Paper Towels or Sponge
Plastic Wrap

Using The Kitchen

BASIC COOKING TECHNIQUES

The primary objective of any form of cooking is to achieve what the French so aptly call, "à point," the ideal state of preparedness of cooked food. Food in this state will have:

1. The proper degree of tenderness

2. The ideal flavor

3. The precise temperature

4. The appropriate texture

5. The perfect aroma

6. An enticing appearance

I cannot guarantee achieving à point in every menu with minimum practice and simply following the guidelines in this book. Achieving that state of cooking nirvana would most likely have your date in such an amorous condition that I would not want to be responsible for the consequences. You can, however, achieve results which will generate more than adequate responses with a minimum of practice.

After a few serious efforts in the kitchen you will readily see that cooking is not the complicated, technical chore you thought it to be. I found cooking to be a lot easier to learn·than tennis, a great deal less painful than running, and, if done properly, almost as healthy as both.

The simple key to becoming a successful cook are the same as those things necessary to achieve success in any endeavor:

1. Follow instructions

2. Practice

3. Enjoy what you are doing

The only variables that can alter the desired results of a recipe are variations in ingredients and differentials in cooking temperatures due to varieties of stoves and utensils. These minor variables will be discovered during practice and can be easily adjusted for by altering cooking times accordingly.

The following outline reviews the different methods of cooking foods and offers helpful hints to minimize problems and maximize results. Not all of these methods of cooking are needed for preparing the menus presented in this book. They are provided as a handy reference when discussing cooking with a knowledgeable date or for those interested in more advanced cooking techniques.

Bake
Baking is a dry heat process where the food is heated by a combination of reflected and radiant heat from the oven and heat transferred directly from the utensil. The moisture is released from the food itself and circulates within the closed oven chamber thereby maintaining some small degree of moistness for the food. In most instances baking is done in a preheated oven and it is most critical that the oven reach the prescribed temperature before the food is placed into it.

To test poultry that is being baked, for the degree of doneness, prick the poultry with a fork and if the juices that rise to the surface are red or pink, the poultry needs more cooking time. When the poultry is done, the juices should be clear and the meat tender when cut.

When baking a cake or pastry that is supposed to rise, do not open the oven to peek until the total baking time has elapsed. To test for doneness, use a broomstraw or a toothpick and insert it into the cake and if nothing sticks to it when it is pulled out, the cake should be done.

In general, baking of cakes, pastries or pies are the most difficult forms of cooking because of the critical nature of preparing the ingredients. In this book I have purposely not introduced any difficult baked goods into any of the menus.

Blanch
There are two basic forms of blanching. One is to pour boiling water over food to aid in removing the skin or outer covering. After the boiling water is poured over the food for about 10 seconds, the food is then plunged into cold water. This process makes the removal of tomato or peach skins much easier. The second is to place the food to be blanched into cold water and bring the water slowly to a boil and continue to simmer for the length of time specified. After the proper cooking time has elapsed, the food is drained and plunged into cold water to terminate the cooking process. A similar process, parboiling, is discussed later in this text.

Boil
Boiling in general means cooking food in a liquid that is highly agitated by high heat and sending up rolling bubbles. Only food requiring quick evaporation, such as in reducing a liquid for a sauce, is ever boiled. In most instances a liquid is brought to a boil, the food to be cooked is introduced, and the temperature is reduced to permit simmering.

Each recipe in this book gives detailed instructions when it requires the use of boiling.

A boiling liquid should always be watched since the agitation can become so great as to cause the hot liquid to spill out of the utensil onto the heating element.

Braise
To sauté foods in fat in order to seal in some of the foods' juices and impart a brown color to the outside of the food. This process does not cook the food through and is used prior to baking in a casserole or other form of cooking.

This process is generally used to prepare meats but in some of the situations is referred to when cooking vegetables in butter.

Broil
Broiling is a dry heat process where only one side of the food at a time is

exposed to the heat source. The heat source is usually very hot and cooking is done fairly quickly. You must carefully check the instructions for your particular stove since some stoves require pre-heating, while others do not; some require the door to be ajar, while for others the door may or must be closed. For proper broiling you must experiment and get to know your stove since broiling temperatures on various models are different. Test any recipes requiring broiling in your stove to determine the exact cooking time to give you the best results. When you have determined the proper timing, adjust your recipes accordingly.

For most recipes the oven rack should be adjusted to position the food 3 inches from the heat source. For very thick meats or delicate sauces, the distance between food and heat source may be 4 to 6 inches.

Brown This term means the same as braise as well as to impart a brown crust or top to baked goods or casseroles by baking at a raised temperature or broiling for a short period of time close to the heating element.

Deglaze To pour liquid, water or wine, into the cooking pan after meat or poultry has been roasted or sautéed and the pan has been degreased and scrape all the flavorful coagulated cooking residue into it as it simmers. This liquid is used to prepare sauces incorporating in them the savory flavor of the meat or poultry from whence they came.

Degrease To remove the fat from the surface of hot liquids in sauces, soups, stocks, roasts, or casseroles. This is done by tilting the pan and skimming the fat off the top of the liquid with a spoon or basting bulb.

Flambé To cause a food to burst dramatically into flames just prior to serving. Brandy is the most common liquid used to flame an entree or dessert. The brandy should be gently warmed in a container placed in heated water prior to pouring it on the food and igniting it with a match. For each of the flaming dishes presented in this book, an alternative for the brandy has been suggested. The alternative is "flambé," which can be purchased from a restaurant supply house. This liquid is recommended to assure a spectacular flame rather than a dismal flicker which can occur if brandy is not properly heated or ignited at the appropriate time.

Fricassee A method of preparing chicken or veal wherein the food is first sauteed in butter, then liquid is added and the food simmers in a self sauce.

Fry To cook in fat over medium high to high temperatures to impart a crisp texture to the food and seal in moisture. There are two techniques, one being deep fat frying where the food is totally submerged in the hot fat and pan-frying where the food is only partially submerged in the hot fat and cooking takes place one side at a time. The key to successful frying is to be certain that the fat is hot enough before introducing the food to be cooked. A simple method of determining proper cooking temperature is to place a bread cube into the fat for 60 seconds and test it for proper cooking characteristics. A frying thermometer is the best method and should always be warmed and completely dry before submersing it into hot fat.

Again, since deep fat frying requires more sophisticated skills as is the case with baking, I have not introduced dishes into the menus in this book requiring this technique.

Be Careful when introducing the food into the hot fat. The fat may splatter causing painful burns.

Pan-broil To cook meat in a pan over a medium to medium high heat without the use of butter, oil or fat. The inside of the pan can be rubbed with a small quantity of fat from the piece of meat to be cooked. The meat usually is seared first in order to seal in the natural juices.

Pan-fry   To cook food, usually breaded or coated with seasoned flour, in a small amount of fat in a fry pan over medium high heat. The food is browned on one side then turned and browned on the other side. The fat must be hot enough before the food is introduced or the fat will be absorbed by the food generating a soggy unappetizing result.

Be Careful when introducing food into the hot fat. The fat may splatter causing painful burns.

Parboil   The food, usually potatoes or vegetables, is plunged into rapidly boiling water and cooked for the period indicated in the recipe. The food is then drained and additional cooking such as casseroling or roasting takes place. This procedure partially cooks foods and sets the color of the food, preserves the nutrients and firms the tissues of the food.

Plank   To cook meat on a 1 inch thick kiln dried oak slab. The meat is usually surrounded by a decorative band of potatoes and garnished with colorful vegetables. The oak slab imparts a delightful flavor to the meat.

Poach   To cook food submerged in a liquid that is barely simmering. This type of cooking produces a self-basting which is constant during the cooking cycle.

Reduce   To boil down a sauce or liquid to concentrate the flavor and thicken the consistency. Usually the liquid is boiled down to half its volume.

Roast   To cook meat on a revolving spit over an open fire. Due to the general unavailability of this equipment most roasting is done in a pan in an oven. Roasting at high heat seals in the juices while roasting at low heat minimizes shrinkage. Roasts should be prepared in special roasting pans or racks to elevate the meat off of the surface of the pan and allow for the sizzling fat to collect. The roast should be basted in its own juices every 15 to 20 minutes to keep the meat moist and tender. A meat thermometer should be inserted into the roast prior to the roast being placed into the pre-heated oven. Most recipes show the appropriate temperature you should achieve on the meat thermometer for the desired degree of doneness. The best grade of Prime or Choice meat should be selected for a roast to assure a tender, succulent result.

Sauté   To brown food in butter or oil and butter until it is cooked to the desired degree of doneness. Fat should be hot and the food dry and warm (70ºF.) before the food is introduced into the pan and the sautéing is started. The food should be constantly moving by stirring or shaking as it is sautéing. Most food to be sautéed is cut into small pieces. Food processed in this manner retains its own juices. This is one of the most important of the primary cooking techniques and should be practiced the most in order to achieve the greatest success with this book.

Scald   To cook at a temperature just below the boiling point. Most often referred to with relation to milk.

Sear   To seal in the juices of foods, usually meat, by cooking over high heat for a short period of time. This process often precedes stewing or casseroling. The indicator as to when one side of the meat has been properly seared is to observe blood rising to the surface of the other side. At this point it is time to turn the meat and sear the other side.

Simmer   To cook food in liquid at a temperature below the boiling point so bubbles occasionally break the surface. Simmering protects fragile foods and tenderizes tough foods.

Steam   To cook food, usually vegetables, in steam rather than liquid. The food is placed into a steamer which raises the food above the boiling water and allows the steam to envelope the food through holes in the steamer. This method of cooking vegetables produces superior flavor and texture.

Stew   To simmer a food in liquid from the start of the cooking process. The primary difference between stewing and fricasseeing is that in fricasseeing, the food is sautéed before being placed into the liquid for simmering and in stewing the food goes directly into the liquid for simmering.

CUTTING

In addition to the obvious practicality of being able to skillfully handle a knife in the kitchen, there is the added benefit of sensuality. Somehow the apparent danger involved in rapidly slicing a vegetable into thin slivers a mere breath away from one's fingers creates an aura of sensuality. This skill as well as those required to prepare a flaming coffee and to french serve are the ones I highly recommend devoting extra time in perfecting. The reason being that the results most definitely justify the added effort. By focusing attention on these few skills, and doing them well, you give your date the impression and assurance that you are a master of all cooking skills. After all, many impressive maitre'd's can perform the later two skills with perfection and cannot even prepare a meal although certainly giving the illusion that they could do so with the verve of a master.

The goal of the Kitchen Casanova is to obtain the maximum results with the minimum of effort. For those times when your date may be present while you are preparing the ingredients for a meal, a skillful technique with the chef's knife is impressive. The following points are critical to developing skill in cutting.

Sharp Knife   Before you can even begin to learn the different techniques of cutting you must be certain your knife is razor sharp. The mainstay of your cutting arsenal is the 8'' chef's knife and your sharpening steel. Before starting any food cutting, a few strokes on the sharpening steel with knife blade forming a 33⁰ angle with steel is in order. A properly sharpened knife when drawn across a tomato should cut through the skin with just the weight of the knife.

Chopping   Hold the knife with your thumb and index finger of your dominant hand gripping the top of the blade just in front of the handle and wrap the other fingers around the handle. Grasp the knife tip with the thumb and index finger of the non-dominant hand and chop with rapid up and down movements, brushing the food repeatedly into a pile with the edge of the knife blade.

Slicing   To slice round objects, cut them in half and lay the cut side down on the cutting board. Long objects such as carrots or celery may be sliced lengthwise and the cut side placed down on the cutting board if necessary for added stability. The cutting procedure involves grasping the knife with the thumb and index finger of the dominant hand and placing the knife point on the cutting board to act as a pivot. The point is never lifted from the cutting board and the cutting edge of the knife is never lifted above the first joint of the forefinger of the hand holding the food. Use the thumb of the holding hand as a pusher, and grip the sides of the food with your fingers, pointing your fingernails back towards your thumb so as not to cut them. The knife blade is raised high enough to clear the top of the food being sliced and then eased down through the food using the knuckles of the forefinger and mid-finger of the holding hand as a guide. With each slice, move the holding hand the distance of a desired cut, retreating along the length of the food. As long as the wide, flat, side of the blade is resting against the knuckles of the two guide fingers and the fingernails are pointing towards the thumb, you cannot cut yourself and the knife will be in good control.

Practice this technique, slowly at first, and pick up speed as you gain confidence. Within a short time you will be ready to give a live perfomance of your cutting skill.

Julienne

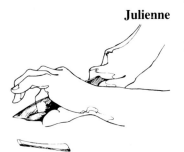

To cut vegetables into julienne strips, cut the vegetables into lengthwise slices 1/8'' thick. Cut these slices into strips 1/8 across and cut the strips into whatever lengths you wish. Usually julienned strips are 1 1/2'' to 2'' in length.

Dicing

Proceed as for julienne strips, then cut the strips, a bunch at a time, crosswise into 1/8'' dice.

MEASURING

Careful measuring of ingredients is important in generating tasty, consistent results. There are no shortcuts to measuring and I certainly don't subscribe to ''a pinch of this and a dash of that''. All quantities in this book are expressed in standard U.S. measures. An accurate set of U.S. Standard measuring cups and U.S. Standard measuring spoons are suggested as Basic Necessities for the Kitchen Casanova kitchen. Always measure all ingredients before you start to cook.

The following are procedures you should use when measuring ingredients.

Bulk Fats Use the displacement method. For 1/3 cup fat, fill the measuring cup with 2/3 cup water. Add fat until the water reaches the 1 cup mark. Drain the water from the cup and the fat remaining will equal 1/3 cup.

Butter or Margarine In stick form, these ingredients usually have measurement marks on the wrapping paper. A 1/4 lb. stick equals 1/2 cup.

Dry Ingredients Fill the appropriate size measuring cup or spoon to overflowing directly from the package. Do not pack down or bang the cup or spoon on the table and level the top with a knife or other flat utensil. When used in baking, flour is usually sifted after measuring. Check your recipe carefully to see whether it specifies sifted ingredients.

Seasonings Fill the appropriate size measuring spoon to over flowing and level the top with a knife or edge of another flat utensil. If a recipe calls for a dash or a pinch, use about half the 1/8 teaspoon measure.

Equivalent Measures

3 teaspoons	equals	1 tablespoon
2 tablespoons	equals	1 fluid ounce
4 tablespoons	equals	1/4 cup or 2 fluid ounces
16 tablespoons	equals	1 cup or 8 fluid ounces
2 cups	equals	1 pint
2 pints	equals	1 quart
4 quarts	equals	1 gallon

FOOD SHOPPING

It is most disheartening when you are preparing a meal to discover that you do not have a certain ingredient. In order to prevent this from happening all you have to do is review the menu you are going to prepare and list all ingredients on a shopping list. Take the list and cross off all the ingredients you can physically find in your kitchen. The remainder of the items will necessitate a trip to the grocery store. Never try to commit to memory what you will need for the menu you have selected. That is a guaranteed way to miss some critical ingredient.

When you write a shopping list do yourself a big favor and group all similar items likely to be found in the same section of the store. Examples of groups are: vegetables, meats, dairy items, spices, fruits and frozen foods.

When shopping, start at one side of the grocery store and work your way systematically to the other side, checking off each item as you place it in your cart.

If you want to economize, check available generic store brands using the unit pricing method of comparison. You will be amazed at some of the savings you can accrue by not buying a name brand. When buying vegetables, meat, poultry or seafood, be sure to buy the best quality and the freshest. A few cents saved in this area can make many dollars difference in taste. If in doubt about a certain cut of meat, don't hesitate to ask the store butcher for assistance.

Another way to economize is to only shop on a full stomach. If you do your shopping when you are extremely hungry you will find there is a great tendancy for impulse buying of things you normally wouldn't buy if your hunger was satisfied. When in doubt, eat first, then shop.

When you get home from shopping be sure to immediately place all refrigerated items and frozen foods in the refrigerator and freezer.

One last pointer for the true Kitchen Casanova, always look forward to grocery shopping because it is an ideal opportunity to meet potential dates. Everyone in your neighborhood eventually must shop for food. If you spot someone who interests you as a potential date, a casual question about a type of produce or a cut of meat is a good opener. If you are particularly intrigued by someone, chances are very good that they will be there the same time next week since most people shop for groceries on a scheduled weekly basis. A word of caution, a true Kitchen Casanova is discreet and a gentleman. Don't be too aggressive or you may quickly acquire the reputation of being the "Supermarket Masher" instead of a Kitchen Casanova.

KITCHEN TIPS

The following tips will help you achieve a smooth and successful preparation of all menus and act as a guide to help you through any unforseen emergencies.

Clean Utensils　Clean utensils and a clean oven distribute heat more evenly than dirty ones and do not impart foreign tastes to the foods being cooked.

Cooking Preparation　Measure all ingredients for each recipe and place them in small bowls, cups or saucers before you start cooking so you won't be rushed when the recipe calls for any ingredients to be added during the cooking process.

Fire　In case of a grease fire NEVER THROW WATER onto it. Douse the fire with salt or baking soda or cover it with a metal lid. A multi-purpose fire extinguisher is a practical item to have in a handy spot in the kitchen.

Flour Sauces　When a recipe calls for flour in a sauce, use an instant flour since it needs no sifting and does not create lumps as easily as regular flour. Instant flour is available at most grocery stores.

Frying　When pan frying, a metal colander can be placed over the pan to prevent grease from splattering onto the stove.

Knives　When you are finished using a knife, rinse it immediately, dry it, and put it in your knife rack. This will prolong the life of the blade and assure a sharp knife when you next need it. If your knives are stainless steel this factor is not as critical.

Onion or Garlic Smell　To remove onion or garlic smell from the hands;

1. Rub the hands with salt

2. Rinse the hands with cold water

3. Repeat 1 and 2

4. Wash hands with warm water and soap

5. Rubbing the hands with a slice of lemon can also help alleviate the onion or garlic smell

Oven Temperature　If there is any doubt as to the accuracy of your oven thermostat use a separate oven thermometer to check the thermostat since many stove thermostats are inaccurate.

Peeling Onions　To avoid tearing when peeling onions, peel them under cold running water. Breathing only through your mouth while peeling and cutting can also inhibit tearing.

Pouring Hot Liquids　When pouring hot liquids into glass, put a metal spoon into the glass and pour the liquid onto the spoon to absorb excess heat and prevent the glass from cracking.

Scorched Pans　To clean a scorched pan first soak the pan in water and dishwashing detergent overnight. If the scorch marks do not come out, boil the pan in a solution of 1 teaspoon baking soda or cream of tartar for each quart of water.

Thickening Sauces　If you are having difficulty getting a sauce to thicken, mix one teaspoon cornstarch in two tablespoons cold water and add the mixture to your sauce.

Wine Cooking　When cooking with wine, if Chablis or a specific dry white wine is specified in the recipe, you can substitute any dry white wine and obtain acceptable results. I recommend using table wines for cooking rather than "cooking wines" since cooking wines contain salt which can alter your balance of seasoning.

GLOSSARY OF BASIC COOKING TERMS

A

Aromatics Ingredients which give flavor and scent to food, e.g. herbs, spices, garlic; whether in cooking or added to a cooked dish.

B

Bake To cook by dry heat, e.g. in an oven.

Baste To moisten meat, poultry or fish with hot fat or liquid as it cooks. Use a large spoon or basting bulb.

Beat To mix foods or liquids thoroughly and vigorously with a circular motion using a spoon, fork or spatula.

Blanch To immerse food in boiling water for a short period of time in order to precook it or facilitate the removal of the skin of the food.

Blend To stir a mixture using a moderate circular motion until it is completely combined and smooth.

Boil To cook in water or liquid at 212°F. at sea level with the liquid bubbling vigorously.

Braise To saute' foods in fat in order to seal in some of the foods' juices and impart a brown color to the outside of the food.

Broil To cook meat, fish, or poultry by direct heat, usually under an electric or gas broiler.

Brown To saute' foods in fat in order to seal in some of the foods' juices and impart a brown color to the outside of the food. Same as braise.

C

Cassoulet A rich combination of beans baked with a variety of meats.

Chop To cut into small uneven pieces with a sharp knife.

Clarified Butter The clear yellow liquid remaining when butter is heated to foaming, then chilled and the milky residue is removed.

Compote Fruit poached in a syrup, usually sugar and water or sugar and wine.

D

Deglaze To pour liquid, water or wine, into the cooking pan after meat or poultry has been roasted or sauteed and scrape all the cooking residue into it as it simmers. A good base for sauces.

Degrease To remove the fat from the surface of hot liquids in sauces, soups, stocks, roasts or casseroles.

Dice To cut food into cubes about 1/8" in size.

Dot To place small pieces of butter on the surface of food, usually prior to broiling or baking in a casserole.

Drizzle To pour a liquid or sauce in a thin stream randomly over top of a food.

E

Entree Any food other than a roast served as the main course of a meal. In France, however, the entree is the appetizer or entry into the main course.

F

Flambé   To cause a food to burst dramatically into flames just prior to serving.

Foam   An aggregation of minute bubbles formed on the surface of a cooking liquid such as butter.

Fold   To mix a light substance with a heavier one so as little lightness as possible is lost. The mixture must be lifted from beneath and folded over, not stirred in a circle.

Fricassee A method of preparing chicken or veal wherein the food is first sauteed in butter, then liquid is added and the food simmers in a self sauce.

Fry   To cook food in fat over medium high to high temperature in order to impart a crisp texture to the food and seal in moisture.

G

Garnish   To decorate as you like in a pleasing fashion.

Grate   To scrape into small pieces by rubbing a hard food like cheese or raw vegetables on a grater.

Gratin (au) To cook food covered in crumbs, butter, sauce or grated cheese in the oven or under the broiler to produce a light brown crust.

Grease   To coat with a thin layer of butter or shortening.

H

Hors d'oeuvre A hot or cold bite sized snack served before a meal usually with a cocktail or wine.

J

Julienne   Fine strips of meat or vegetables, usually about 1/8'' to 1/4'' thick by 2'' long.

M

Marinate   To soak raw meat, fish or poultry in a chilled cooked or uncooked spiced liquid of wine, oil, herbs and vegetables for hours before cooking. This process tenderizes and flavors the meat, fish or poultry.

Mince   To cut or chop into as small pieces as possible.

Mousse   A sweet, smooth mixture, airy but rich, made from eggs, sugar, cream and flavorings. Usually served chilled. Powdered gelatin may be used for setting.

P

Pan-broil To cook meat in a pan over medium to medium high heat without the use of butter, oil or fat.

Pan-fry   To cook food, usually breaded or coated with seasoned flour, in a small amount of fat in a pan over medium to medium high heat.

Parboil   To boil until partially cooked, as with potatoes or vegetables prior to cooking in casseroles or roasting.

Plank   To cook meat on a 1'' thick kiln dried oak slab.

Poach   To cook food submerged in a liquid that is barely simmering.

R

Reduce   To boil down a sauce or liquid to concentrate the flavor and thicken the consistency.

Roast   To cook meat on a revolving spit over an open fire or in a roasting pan in an oven.

S

Sauté   To brown food in butter or oil and butter until cooked to the desired degree of doneness while stirring or shaking constantly.

Scald   To cook at a temperature just below the boiling point.

Score   To make a series of shallow, even cuts.

Sear   To seal in the juices of foods, usually meat, by cooking over high heat for a short period of time.

Shred   To cut or break into uneven strips.

Simmer   To cook in liquid at 195ºF. (low heat) or just below the boiling point so bubbles occasionally break the surface of the liquid.

Slice   To cut food to a specified thickness with a knife.

Steam   To cook food, usually vegetables, in steam rather than liquid. Creates flavorful, healthy vegetables.

Stew   To simmer a food in liquid from the start of the cooking process.

Stir   To mix using a continuous circular motion.

T

Tenderize   To break down tough fibers in meat by heating, marinating, or beating with a mallet.

W

Whisk   To beat fast with a circular motion so that a mixture is made lighter by incorporating air into it.

Meal Presentation

MOOD

Next to proper preparation and flavor of a meal, a romantic mood is the most important element of a Kitchen Casanova dinner. Just as it takes a proper blending of ingredients with perfect timing to prepare a delicious meal, so it takes a proper blending of many factors and perfect timing to create a romantic atmosphere. We must never lose sight of the fact that the primary objective of the Kitchen Casanova is to create the most enjoyable dining experience possible. Your date must be utterly relaxed and prepared to absorb the sights, sounds, tastes and subtle tactile experiences that embody a pleasureable happening.

The following are elements that all contribute to a truly romantic atmosphere.

Manners   From the moment you arrive to pick up your date, or, under our ever expanding feminist state, when your date arrives, proper manners are critical. Take your date's coat, tell her how beautiful she looks, comment on her clothes or perfume and offer her wine, a cocktail or a non-alcoholic drink. If your date smokes, be sure to offer to light her cigarette and provide an ashtray. If your home or apartment is presentable, and it should be, offer to give her a tour to help her feel at home. If she is about to be seated or is about to arise from the table, be sure to assist her with her chair. Whenever possible, help her feel feminine and special. It is always proper to ask your date after she has accepted a dinner invitation if she has any favorite foods or if there are certain foods she cannot eat or does not care for.

Drinks   If you plan to serve wine, cocktails or a nonalcoholic beverage before the meal, have all the glasses and necessary mixes ready on a tray. Cracked ice should be ready in an ice bucket and only handled with tongs or a scoop.

Hors d'oeuvres   Light Hors d'oeuvres such as crackers and a variety of cheeses is a pleasant way to begin the evening. For a bit more flair you may want to try your hand at making a few fancy hors d'oeuvres or buy some frozen ones at the gourmet section of your supermarket and heat them when your date arrives. Fresh vegetables such as carrot sticks, broccoli, cauliflower or mushrooms and a sour cream dip make a very appetizing hors d'oeuvre.

Hired Help   For the ultimate in entertaining, if your budget permits, you may desire to hire a waiter or waitress to serve the meal and clean up afterwards. This method definitely succeeds in making your date feel special. Be sure that the help leaves before the Après Dining activities. If you have a roommate you may want to enter into a reciprocal arrangement where you act as waiter for his dates and he acts as waiter for your dates. This added touch may be costly but is definitely impressive.

Relaxed Atmosphere   The most important factor is to make your date feel totally relaxed. Asking her to select the mood music is a good way to help her feel a part of the evening. The most successful method of establishing a relaxed atmosphere is good conversation over a glass of wine before dinner. From time to time as your recipes necessitate your attention in the kitchen, invite your date to join you as you put the finishing touches on each dish. Be sure the kitchen is neat and clean and that any special cooking skills required have been sufficiently mastered before making the invitation. By all means if your date offers to assist in preparing the meal, thank her for her offer but remind her that this is her special evening and her job is to relax and enjoy herself. You cannot expect your date to be relaxed if you are nervous and apprehensive. At all times be a professional in your cooking and entertaining role. The basic difference between a professional and an amateur, aside from skill, is an air of confidence. A successful Kitchen Casanova is cool and confident.

Lighting   Lighting plays a key role in establishing the romantic mood. An inexpensive light dimmer should be installed for your dining room lights. If you dine in a kitchenette, the light fixture over the table should be on a dimmer switch. Prior to your date's arrival, the lighting in the dining area should be subdued. Just prior to serving dinner, the candles, which are an integral part of the table setting, should be lit and the lighting dimmed very low or preferrabley extinguished. Flickering candle light, as well as having a soothing effect on sensitive nerves, improves the rich glow of most foods.

Music   The romantic trinity is formed by wine, soft candlelight and music. Whether classical strings or lovers' ballads, background music should be playing when your date arrives. Tapes, albums or a good FM station can fill the bill. Be sure not to blast the volume and drown out any good conversation. The music is strictly background, but very important background. Find out your date's preference in music and provide it if at all possible. You should set up your music so you will not have to be changing records or tapes during the dinner. A reel to reel tape system is ideal for recording a repertoire of background music custom selected for your special date.

Fragrance   A fresh pleasing aroma adds to a romantic mood. The fragrant smell of fresh cut flowers can enhance any mood. If fresh flowers are not available, a subtle incense can lighten the air in the dining room. Be careful not to overpower or counteract the natural aroma of the meal as this would be counterproductive. Even a single rose will provide a refreshing lift to the air.

Temperature   A too hot or too cold room will detract from the proper mood. Even with today's energy conservation standards, 68°F. to 70°F. should provide an acceptable temperature. Ask your date if she is comfortable at the room temperature and offer to change it to suite her comfort.

TABLE SETTING

A great stumbling block for many budding Kitchen Casanovas is encountered in preparing the dining table for an entertaining meal. Where do the forks go? Does the wine glass go to the right or left of the water glass? Do I serve from the left and remove plates from the right, or vice versa? How do those fancy waiters serve with a fork and spoon in the same hand?

If these questions have gone through your mind and caused you to hesitate in inviting a date for a cozy dinner at your place, fear not, for the answer to those and other points of etiquette are answered below.

The Table Always protect a hardwood table top from heat damage by using table pads. These can be purchased at most department stores in the housewares department. If a pad is not available, a double table cloth will offer some protection.

Table Cloth A table cloth and coordinated cloth napkins are necessary when entertaining and can go a long way in enhancing a battered old dining table.

Centerpiece A pleasing centerpiece is a dramatic focal point for a table setting. The centerpiece should be low or lacy as not to interrupt the view of your date. The following are some examples of possible centerpieces:

Fruit and Nuts in a Bowl
Dried Flower Arrangement
Silk Flower Arrangement
A Single Rose in a Bud Vase
Fresh Flowers
A Pleasant Piece of Sculpture Surrounded by Greens
A Live Plant in a Sculptured Planter

Your local department store, florist or gift shop can assist you in selecting a suitable centerpiece.

Candles Always have candles for your intimate dinners. Nothing enhances a romantic atmosphere like soft, flickering candlelight. Two candles, one on either side of your centerpiece, should be your standard fare. Tall tapers accent most settings the best, but any candle can serve the purpose if it is properly coordinated with your table setting. If a taper has been previously used, by all means go for the extra dollar or two and have two new candles on the table for your special date. You wouldn't want your date to spend the evening wondering who got the first use out of the candles.

Silver or Stainless Forks are to the left of the dinner plate except for the tiny seafood fork which goes on the right. Spoons, including iced-tea spoons, and knives go to the right of the dinner plate, with the knife next to the plate with its sharp blade pointing toward the plate. The utensils to be used first should be placed fartherest from the plate. Never have more than 3 pieces of silver at either side of the plate. If additional items are needed, bring them to the table as the course requiring them is served. Line the base of the handles up about one inch from the edge of the table. The dessert spoon and fork may be placed above the plate with the base of the spoon to the right and the fork above the spoon with its base to the left. An alternative is to bring the dessert spoon and fork to the table when the dessert is served.

Napkin The napkin should be linen or cloth and pressed for the occasion. The napkin is placed folded or in a ring to the far left of the forks or on the dinner plate. An alternative to this is to learn a fancy folding technique and place the napkin in the empty water glass. With this technique, when your date takes her napkin out of the water glass you must immediately fill it.

Glasses The water glass is placed to the upper right of the dinner plate and 3/4 filled with ice water. A sprig of fresh mint or a twist of lemon is a pleasant enhancement when placed in each water glass. The empty wine glass, large bowl for red and small bowl for white, is to the right of the water glass. Glasses are always handled by the stem. Water and wine are poured from the right side of your date. When serving wine, a chilled bottle should be wrapped in a napkin and another napkin should be held in the pourer's left hand to catch any drips. As you finish pouring wine from a bottle, a slight twist of the hand as the neck of the bottle is raised helps to minimize any dripping.

Plates   The salad plate or bowl is placed to the upper left of the dinner plate. A bread and butter plate is slightly above and to the right of the salad plate. Plates are removed from the right and placed from the left of your date.

Tea or Coffee   When it is time to serve tea or coffee, the empty cup and saucer are placed to your date's right. A spoon is on the saucer behind the cup with the base pointing to the right. The cup handle is turned to your date's right. Sugar and cream are offered from the left.

SERVING

Once you have created the proper mood and established the correct table setting, it is important that you correctly serve the meal to your date. Always serve from the left of your date. Whenever passing a serving dish to your date, be sure that the handles of the serving utensils are directed towards her.

If you are having assistance in the kitchen and in serving, then the salad can be served before the main course. If you are the chef and waiter, then it is perfectly acceptable for you to serve the salad, pour the wine and serve the main course before sitting down to enjoy the meal with your date. If the meal is such that the main course can be cooking unattended while you and your date enjoy your salads, then ask your date if she would care to have her salad before or during the main course and plan accordingly.

French Serve   This technique of serving used by all premier class waiters is very impressive indeed when used to serve the meal to your date. Before using this technique it should be practiced until you can use it comfortably with confidence. This technique involves the use of a fork and serving spoon simultaneously and is performed as follows:

1. With the dominant hand open in the palm up position, place the serving fork over the middle finger, under the ring finger and over the little finger and hold securely by slightly flexing the fingers.
2. Grasp the serving spoon with the thumb and index finger of the same hand.
3. To serve meats, fish, poultry or firm vegetables, slide the fork under the food and grip the food using the spoon to clamp it in place against the fork while transporting it to the dinner plate.
4. To serve sauces or soft liquid foods, use the spoon while holding the fork to the side.
5. This technique will feel very awkward at first, somewhat similar to learning to use chop sticks. Practice whenever you get a chance and you will find the technique will become more and more comfortable.

Wine

Nothing enhances a romantic atmosphere of candlelight and soft music like the coupling of a delectable meal, cooked to perfection and served so that it is as seductive to the eye as to the appetite, and a shimmering glass of wine. The soft glow of a gleaming red or the rich golden highlights of a white reflecting the essence of candlelight warms the senses and stimulates the imagination. The flavor and aroma of wine can be the catalyst to enhance a fine meal into a memorable experience.

Knowledge of wine is oft-times shrouded in mystery and thought only to be for the creme-de-creme of society. A basic knowledge of wine does not necessitate years of study at the Sorbonne and countless nights visiting the estates of France. After all, is wine not simply formented grapes? I can hear the gnashing of teeth of the great wine connoisseurs upon reading the previous statement. Certainly a great deal of care and infinite controls are necessary to both grow the vintage grapes and transform them into the nectar of the gods.

SELECTING THE PROPER WINE

The important factors which determine a superior wine are the soil, climate, vine-type and the winemaker. If one wishes to become an expert in wines, then it will be necessary to research and study the vintage wine charts for each major wine producer and, through much tasting, instruction and patience, develop the palate to truly distinguish the superb from the great.

The primary criteria in selecting a wine is whether or not the wine pleases you. An experienced wine merchant can assist in educating you as to qualities of various wines. I suggest that if you are interested in becoming knowledgeable about wines, you select a new wine each week and study its background. Learn the history of the winery, vineyard and region from where it comes. Make notes as to the flavor and bouquet of the wine and rate it as to your personal preference. Keep this information in a notebook for future reference. Attend wine tasting parties as this will assist in broadening your experience with the many varieties and qualities of wines. Within a short period of time you will begin to gain an insight into the many facets of this enchanting of all drinks.

Each Kitchen Casanova menu lists a suggested wine by general category or region. It is up to you to select the specific wine from within this category which can vary considerably according to price. You will be surprised to find that not always the most expensive wine will be your particular favorite. Since wine is a truly personal pleasure, you may desire to substitute your own special wine, which is, of course, acceptable.

In general, the more specific the location stated on the wine label where the wine was grown and bottled, the better the wine. For the purpose of this book, the following section offers a short review of some of the wines of France, Italy, Germany and the United States.

THE WINES OF FRANCE

The most famous of the winemaking countries is unmistakably France. The most magnificent wines in the world come from this nation known for it's countless contributions to the arts. The winemakers take their place beside the great painters and sculptors.

Wine	Region	Vineyard	Characteristics	Serve With
BORDEAUX bôr dō′	Graves grav	Château Haut-Brion	Vigorous, full-bodied, long lasting reds and from dry to sweet whites.	Turkey Chicken Lamb Duck Steaks Spiced dishes Beef
	Médoc mā dòk′	Château Lafite Rothschild	One of the greatest red Bordeaux. This wine has a unique softness and exquisite bouquet. This wine is slow to mature and should not be drunk too young.	Turkey Chicken Lamb Duck Steaks Spiced dishes Beef
		Château Mouton-Rothschild	Very similar to the Lafite Rothschild.	Same as Above
	Pomerol pôm a rôl′	Château Pétrus	A sturdy wine with a finesse and subtlety to its flavor.	Same as Above
	St.Emilion san tā mē lyôn′	Château Ausone	Big red wines, somewhat similar to Burgandies. Full rich bodied wines which are slow to mature. These wines shouldn't be drunk too young.	Turkey Chicken Lamb Duck Steaks Spiced dishes Beef
		Château Cheval-Blanc		
	Sauternes sô tern′	Château d'Yquem	Sweet white wines made by slight over-ripening of the grapes	Desserts Hors d' oeuvres
		Château Guiraud	These wines should be served cold but not overchilled.	Sweet fish dishes.

Wine	Region	Vineyard	Characteristics	Serve With
BURGUNDY boŏr'goŏn dē	Côte de Beaune kōt de bōń	Bâtard-Montrachet	One of the greatest of all white Burgundies. Dry and firm but never hard. This wine has a lingering aftertaste.	Poached fish
	Chablis sha blē´	Blanchots Les Clos Chablis-Montée de Tonnerre	Best are pale straw in color with a delicate bouquet and a flinty dry taste. These wines should be drunk young.	Aperitif Fish dish Shellfish Light chicken dishes Veal

(Chablis without any further qualification, means a wine from one of the slopes of the district but not one of the outstanding ones.)

Wine	Region	Vineyard	Characteristics	Serve With
	Côte de Nuits kōt de nwē´	Chambertin	Magnificent and noble red wine. This wine is big and sturdy with a strong color. The wine has a tremendous "nose" or bouquet with a pronounced aftertaste. From a good year this wine is unsurpassed.	Chicken in red sauce Beef Lamb Steaks
	Beaujolais bó shô lé	Moulin-à-Vent	A big red wine with a taste of flowers or fruit and a spicy bouquet. This wine has a very fresh character and should be drunk quite young. The wine can be slightly chilled.	Beef Veal Chicken roasted or braised Good picnic wine
	Maconnais mä kô né	Pouilly-Fuissé	The finest light dry wine of the southern Burgundy. Very pleasant taste with a forthright round fullness. This wine has a pale golden color with overtones of green.	Lobster Shellfish Veal Light chicken dishes

Wine	Region	Vineyard	Characteristics	Serve With
CHAMPAGNE sham pān′		Ambonnay Ay-Champagne Some excellent shipping firms which make champagnes are: Piper-Heidsieck Charles Heidsieck Mumm Taittinger Moët et Chandon Bollinger	Most generally sparkling wines for festive oc- caisions served well chilled. Since the growers seldom vinify their own grapes the vineyard name will not help in selecting a quality champagne.	Caviar Aperitif Salmon Chicken Ham Turkey Seafood Generally with most foods
ALSACE al sās′	Rhine rīn	Vineyard names are not as important here since the wines are named for the grape variety, Riesling.	Sharp, exception- ally dry and fresh white wine.	Fish dishes Pork Aperitif
LOIRE lwar	Brittany brī′ tan ē	Saint-Herblon Vallet Gorges	Very light and dry white wines. These are lovely summer wines when chilled. These wines should be drunk quite young.	Cold fish Shellfish Veal Any Fish dish
	Touraine too reń′	Vouvray (The town or com- mune is listed in lieu of vineyard.)	A light, delightful dry white wine that has a tendancy to- wards sweetness.	Sausage Pork Veal Chicken Sweet Fish dishes
RHONE rōn	Château- neuf-du-Pape shä tō noef′ dy pap′	Domaine des Fines Roches Clos Saint-Jean La Gardine	A stout and robust red wine with full flavor. The Rhone's finest red wine with the most stringent controls in all the world.	Hearty dishes such as stews Game Duck Beef
	Tavel ta vel′	Les Vignerons de Tavel	A full-bodied and sturdy pink color- ed wine. Commonly referred to in the U.S. as Rosé. This wine should be well chilled and young.	Cold dishes Hearty chicken dishes Veal Good picnic wine

THE WINES OF ITALY

Italy is the largest producer and exporter of wine in the world. Italian wines reflect her people in that they are hearty and robust. Due to lax government controls, there are a broad spectrum of wine qualities from rough, tart wines to the excellent delicate Soaves. Italian wines are now controlled by government recognition of three quality standards:

1. Simple (Denominazione di Origine Semplice)
2. Controlled (Denominazione di Origine Controllata,D.O.C.)
3. Controlled and Guaranteed (Denominazione di Origine Controllata e Garantita)

Since controls are not manditory it is important to carefully read the labels on Italian wines before making a purchase.

Wine	Region	Vineyard	Characteristics	Serve With
TUSCANY tuś kan ē	Chianti kyäń tē	Classico Rufina	Agreeable wines but not what one would call distinguished.	Classic Italian dishes

(True Chianti can be distinguished by the seal portraying a black cockerel on a gold background with a surrounding red circle.)

Wine	Region	Vineyard	Characteristics	Serve With
VENETO vé ne tô	Soave swä ve	Town of Soave Town of Monteforte d' Alpone	These wines are light straw in color with greenish highlights. The wines are dry with a slight acid taste and a small but pleasant bouquet.	Pasta dishes with white sauce Veal Chicken dishes
	Valpolicella väĺ pô lē cheí lä	Valpantena Valpolicella	This wine has a delicate bouquet and a rich mouth filling texture. This red wine can be lightly chilled.	Pasta dishes with red sauce Chicken dishes

THE WINES OF GERMANY

In Germany there are many thousands of individual vineyards. As in France, the wines are named for the location from which the grapes were grown and the wine produced. The location is identified by the following subdivisions:

Region (bestimmten Anbaugebiete), sub-region (Bereich), large site (Grosslagen), and vineyard (Einzellagen). The quality of the German wines are divided into three categories:

1. Table Wine (Deutscher Tafelwein)
2. Quality Wine (Qualitatswein bestimmten Anbaugebiet)

3.   Quality Wine with Special Attributes (Qualitatswein mit Pradikat)

The best German white wine grape is the Riesling. This grape variety is not always named on the label of all high quality wines but, unless otherwise designated, the grape variety can be assumed to be Riesling. Practically all of the Mosel region wines come from the Riesling grape variety.

Region	Large Site	Vineyard	Characteristics	Serve With
MOSEL-SAAR-RUWER mō′zel sär roo′ vär	Badstube	Bernkasteler Doctor	Most famous Mosel wine. Light white wine with delicate quality and incomparable bouquet.	Shellfish Fish dishes Veal
		Graben	Very similar to the Doctor wine	Same as Above
		Piesport	This wine is full with a spicy touch.	Same as Above
	Schwarze Katz	Burglay-Felson Pommerell	Not quite the delicate quality of the Bernkastel wines but pleasant dinner wines nevertheless.	Shellfish Fish dishes Veal
RHEINHESSEN rīn′hes′ en	Nierstein	Glock Holle	Soft but full-bodied wines with a beautiful bouquet.	Shellfish Fish dishes Veal

Any quality wine from the Rheinhessen region can be called Liebfraumilch. Most Liebfraumilch is a shipper's blend of the less than the top quality wines from this region. Liebfraumilch has become very popular in the U.S. as a white table wine.

THE WINES OF THE UNITED STATES

The United States has never been looked upon as producer of wines of distinction. In the past few years, however, the U.S. has made giant inroads in gaining the much deserved distinction of producing very palatable and even distinguished wines. In California the climate and soil conditions are equal to those in the best vine-producing regions in France. Acceptable table wines are produced in as diverse states as Arkansas, New York, Ohio, Pennsylvania and New Jersey.

In the United States most of the best wines are named for the dominant grape used in producing the wine rather than only the vineyard name. These wines are called varietals and are usually superior to the wines borrowing the name of a region in France.

The following are a sampling of some of the U.S. wines:

Grape Name	Region	Characteristics	Serve With
CABERNET SAUVIGNON ka ber ne′ sō vē nyôn′	California Varietal	Full-bodied red wine with a medium bouquet. This is the same grape from which most of the great French Bordeaux are made. Superior wines are produced in the Napa, Sonoma and Santa Clara counties of California.	Beef stews Roast chicken Tomato dishes Steaks
CATAWBA ka tä′ ba	New York State, Ohio, and Pennsylvania Varietal	The most widely used native wine grape in the U.S. Produces a pleasant tasting medium white table wine.	Veal Sweet fish dishes Light chicken dishes
GRENACHE gre nash′	California Varietal	Produced as Grenache Rose with a light refreshing sweet flavor and a distinctive bouquet. The finest and most popular is the Grenach Rose from the Almeden Vineyards in Santa Clara county California.	Ham Veal Cold dishes Good picnic wine Good all-around wine
PINOT CHARDONNAY pē nō′ shar dô ne′	California Varietal	A light, delightful, and well balanced white wine. The same grape variety used for the French Chablis and White Burgundies. This wine comes from the Napa, San Benito, Sonoma, and Monterey counties of California.	Ham Turkey Fish Light chicken dishes
PINOT NOIR pē nō nwar′	California Varietal	This grape does not produce as successfully as the Caber-Sauvignon. A big and sturdy red wine with fine color. The finest wines come from the Napa, Sonoma, Monterey, Mendocino and Lake counties of California.	Beef Lamb Cheese Steak

Grape Name	Region	Characteristics	Serve With
SAUVIGNON BLANC sō vē nyôn blän′	California Varietal	This white wine ranges from sweet to dry and is rich and aromatic. The best wines come from the Napa and Sonoma counties of California.	Hors d' oeuvres Veal Light chicken dishes

SERVING WINE

Preparation

White Wines   Serve chilled, the sweeter the wine the colder.

Pink Wines   Serve chilled.

Red Wines   Serve at room temperature, 68ºF to 70ºF.

Old Red Wines   Stand the bottle upright for a few hours before serving so that the sediment settles to the bottom of the bottle.

Young Red Wines   These wines should be uncorked several hours before dinner and, if possible, the day before.

The definition of a young wine varies as per region. A good vintage Bordeaux is classified young when less than 4 years old while a vintage Burgundy is classified young if it is less than 2 1/2 years old.

Glasses   Plain crystal is best, and the larger the bowl and thinner the glass, the better. Good crystal enhances the sparkle of a good wine. There should be room for the wine to be swirled around and to allow it to breathe. In general, glasses with larger bowls are for red wine and glasses with smaller bowls are for white wines. Champagne should be served in a tulip shaped glass not in the classical shallow ''champagne glass'' in order to preserve the sparkling bubbles.

Opening   Cut the capsule and tinfoil below the lip with a sharp knife. Use a clean cloth or napkin to remove the mold which usually forms under the capsule. Pull out the cork and carefully clean the inside of the lip of the bottle. When inserting the corkscrew into the cork, be careful not to turn it through the bottom of the cork as that may cause cork particles to fall into the wine.

For Champagne, let the cork come out slowly into your hand rather than letting it fly into the air with a popping noise. This preserves the precious bubbles that give Champagne its special quality.

Pouring   Wine is always poured from the right side of your date. When serving a chilled wine, the bottle should be wrapped in a napkin and a napkin should be held in the left hand to catch any drips. Wine should always be poured in a continuous motion with a bit of gusto to help it aerate as it flows into the glass. The glass should never be filled more than half full to allow proper room for the wine to breathe. As you finish pouring the wine, a slight twist of the hand as the neck of the bottle is raised helps to minimize any dripping.

APERITIFS

Drinks taken before the meal in order to prepare the palate and stimulate the appetite. Examples of some popular aperitifs are:

Aperitif	Country	Characteristics	Served
Compari	Italy	Bitter flavor	Straight With Soda With Sweet Vermouth
Dry Sherry	Spain	Dry flavor with just a hint of almond.	Straight With Ice
Dry Vermouth	France Italy	Dry flavor with strong herbal taste.	Straight With Ice With Lemon Twist With Soda
Dubonnet	France	Sweet and rather cloying flavor. Comes in dark or blond varieties.	Straight With Ice With Soda
Kir	France	A mixture of white Burgundy and a bit of Cassis, a sweet dark red liqueur made from black-currants.	Straight
Sweet Vermouth	France Italy	Dark in color with a sweet herbal flavor.	Straight With Ice With Lemon Twist With Soda
White Wine	France U.S.	Preferrably dry such as Chablis. Should be well chilled.	Straight

LIQUEURS OR CORDIALS

Sweet, usually strongly alcoholic drinks made of sugar, syrup and spirits, flavored with plants, fruits or herbs. These drinks are usually served after dinner as an aid to digestion.

Liqueur	Country	Characteristics	Served
Anisette	France U.S. Netherlands	Anise flavor	Straight With Ice
Bénédictine	France	Aromatic herbs on a base of Brandy	Straight With Coffee
Bénédictine and Brandy	France	Aromatic herbs with additional Brandy to reduce the sweetness	Straight With Coffee

Liqueur	Country	Characteristics	Served
Cherry Herring	Denmark	Cherry flavored but not too sweet	Straight With Soda With Lime and Tonic
Cognac	France	Brandy which is a distilled wine	Straight
Crème de Cacao	France U.S. Netherlands	Cocoa flavor	Straight
Crème de Cassis	France	Black currant flavor	With Soda With Vermouth With Cognac With White Wine
Crème de Menthe	France U.S. Netherlands	Mint flavor	Straight With Shaved Ice
Curaçao (Cointreau) (Grand Marnier) (Triple Sec)	France U.S.	Orange flavor	Straight Half & Half with Cognac
Drambuie	Scotland	Scotch whiskey and honey	Straight
Irish Mist	Ireland	Irish whiskey and honey	Straight
Ouzo	Greece	Anise flavor	Straight With Water
Slivovitz	Yugoslavia	Plum Brandy	Straight Iced
Strega	Italy	Herbs and citrus flavor	Straight With Coffee
Tia Maria	Jamaica	Coffee flavor	Straight With Coffee

GLOSSARY OF WINE TERMS

Aperitif
Generalized term for almost any drink taken before a meal. The purpose of the aperitif is to prepare the palate and stimulate the appetite.

Appellation Contrôlée
Indicates that the wine has been under the strict laws of the location and conforms to minimum standards as set forth by the French government.

Aroma
The odor of a wine which lingers after the original scent of the bouquet. This odor is usually created directly from the smell of the fruit from which the wine was made.

Body
The substance of wine which fills the mouth with flavor.

Bouquet
The scent of a wine produced by the vaporization of esthers and ethers within the wine. The first scent is the bouquet and the later, more lingering odor, is the aroma.

Carafe
A decanter or glass bottle for serving wines.

Cordial
A drink created from spirits with fruit or aromatic substances added for flavor. They are always sweetened.

Decant
To pour off gently from one container to another as not to disturb the settlement. Wine should be poured in one continuous motion from the bottle to the decanter until the sediment begins to rise to the neck of the bottle.

Dry
The opposite to sweetness. All the sugar has been fermented into alcohol and the resultant flavor is dry.

Flowery
A taste reminiscent of flowers found in young wines. The younger the wine, the more flowery it is apt to be. Few great wines have this quality.

Hard
A drawback to young wines which causes a not too delicate flavor. Usually this flavor turns to a more refined firmness in old age.

Heavy
Very full-bodied, but without distinction. Less negative than coarse which infers no character whatever.

Laws of Classification
A set of classifications established by the French government to rate vineyards in the Bordeaux region.
Grand Cru — Great growths
Premiers Cru — 1st growths
Seconds Cru — 2nd growths

Liqueur
A sweet, strongly alcoholic drink made of sugar and spirits, flavored with plants, fruits or herbs. These drinks are usually consumed after dinner as an aid to digestion.

Mache
A term for wine which tastes tired. The wine tastes as though it were mashed up from chewing.

Mis en Bouteilles au Chateau
French for Chateau bottled. This indicates that the wine was bottled at the vineyards where the wine grapes were grown. Guarantees the authenticity of the wine.

Mis en Bouteilles au Domaine
Same as Mis en Bouteilles au Château.

Palate
The sense of taste. A refined term for taste.

Red Wines
Wines red in color that have light to full-bodied robustness and infinite variety of tastes due to soil and climatic conditions.

Spirits
Alcoholic liquids obtained through distillation.

Thin
A watery poor wine, one that lacks alcoholic content, flavor and body.

Varietal
Wines named for the dominant grape variety.

V.S.O.
Of Cognacs, this means Very Special Old.

V.S.O.P.
Of Cognacs, this means Very Superior Old Pale.

V.V.S.O.P.
Of Cognacs, this means Very, Very Special Old Pale.

Dinner Menus

The following menus have been designed to offer a broad variety of foods covering the basic groups of meat, poultry and seafood. The detailed lists of ingredients can be used for shopping, the timetables and preparation instructions will assure a timely and tasty completion of each menu and the detailed color photographs can be invaluable in garnishing and presenting the menus.

Prepare ingredients refers to cutting and measuring out proper amounts of ingredients. Measured amounts of ingredients can be placed in small juice or shot glasses or on a saucer. When salt, pepper and other spices are called for they can be measured and placed separately in small piles on a saucer.

Read through each recipe before starting to allow sufficient time to familiarize yourself with all techniques required.

IMPORTANT — Before starting any menus be sure to take all required ingredients and place them in an easy to reach common location. This will allow you to achieve the times allowed in the timetable.

BON APPETIT

Menus

Meat Dishes

Tournedos Creme Rouge 44
    Tossed Salad
    Broccoli Amandine
    Baked Potato with Sour Cream
      and Chives
    Fruit Compote Ala Port
    Chateauneuf-du-Pape Wine

Piquant K-Bobs 48
    Pistachio Rice Salad
    Cherries Jubilee
    Medoc Wine

Beef Stroganoff 52
    Mixed Garden Salad
    Broccoli in Lemon Butter Sauce
    Buttered Noodles
    Strawberries Romanoff
    Grenache Rose′ Wine

Beef Bourguignonne Flambe′ 56
    Spinach Salad
    Parsleyed Rice
    Simply Cheese Cake
    Côte de Nuits Wine

Flank Steak with Herb Stuffing 60
    Cucumber Salad
    Potato Parmesan
    Creme de Cafe
    St. Emilion Wine

Veal in Wine Sauce 64
    Mixed Garden Salad
    Tarragon Carrots
    Parsleyed Rice
    Yogurt Apple Pie
    Maconnais Wine

Veal Sinatra 68
    Caesar Salad
    Linguini in White Sauce
    Lemon Mousse
    Medoc Wine

Poultry Dishes

Chicken Cordon Bleu 72
    Spinach Salad
    Baked Pineapple Rice
    Glazed Apples Rose′
    Sauvignon Wine

Breast of Chicken Piccante 76
  Country Salad
  Glazed Carrots
  Parsleyed Rice
  Banana Cream Crunch
  Chablis Wine

Paprika Chicken 80
  Green Salad Supreme
  Ratatouille
  Buttered Noodles
  Strawberries Michele
  Brittany Wine

Coq Au Vin 84
  Tomatoes Gervais
  Rum Peaches
  Pinot Chardonnay Wine

Brandied Chicken Breasts 88
  Spinach Salad
  Tomatoes Au Gratin
  Wild and Nutty Rice
  Pineapple Delight
  Graves Wine

Seafood Dishes

Scallops in Wine Sauce 92
  Tomato Herbal Salad
  Spinach Pie Ala Lilly
  Fruit with Honey Sauce
  Côte de Beaune Wine

Shrimp Sarapico 96
  Orange/Cucumber Salad
  Green Beans Amandine
  Sauternes Rice
  Strawberry Champagne Sherbet
  Granache Rose′ Wine

Flounder Vegetal 100
  Nutty Apple Grape Salad
  Sherried Orange Rice
  Amaretto Delight
  Rhine Wine

Sole Elegante 104
  Pineapple Salad
  Cauliflower in Parsley Butter
  Sauternes Rice
  Alpine Green
  Bernkastel Wine

Menu

Tournedos Crème Rouge

Tossed Salad

Broccoli Amandine

Baked Potatoes with Sour Cream and Chives

Fruit Compote Ala Port

Châteauneuf-du-Pape Wine

Tournedos Crème Rouge

TOURNEDOS CREME ROUGE

Ingredients:		METRIC
1-1/4	lbs. Filet Mignon	.5 kg.
2	tablespoons butter	30 g.
1/2	tablespoon chopped shallots	5 g.
1	teaspoon flour	3 g.
1/2	teaspoon lemon juice	2 ml.
1/2	cup dry Red Wine	125 ml.
1/8	teaspoon salt	.5 ml.
1/8	teaspoon pepper	.5 ml.
1	tablespoon heavy cream	15 ml.
1/2	teaspoon chopped parsley	2 ml.

Preparation:

Panbroil filets: trim any excess fat from the steaks and score the edges with a sharp knife. Rub the inside of a medium fry pan with a small quantity of fat. Preheat the fry pan over medium high heat until a drop of water sizzles when dropped onto the pan. Place the filets into the pan and sear one side until the blood rises to the surface, 1 to 2 minutes. Then turn the filets at once and sear the other side. Reduce the heat to medium and continue to cook the meat uncovered. For a 1-1/2 inch/4 cm. thick steak a cooking time of about 10 minutes should produce a medium well done steak. Cut a filet to check degree of doneness: red inside-rare; pink inside-medium; brown inside-well done. Remove the steaks with their pan juices onto a heated platter.

Heat butter in fry pan over a medium high heat until it foams. Add chopped shallots and sauté until they are light brown. Blend in the flour, stirring constantly, add wine, lemon juice, salt and pepper and simmer on medium heat until the liquid is reduced to about 1/4 cup/60 ml. Stir in the cream and simmer about one minute longer. Spoon the sauce onto the filets, sprinkle with chopped parsley and serve.

TOSSED SALAD

Ingredients:		METRIC
1	small head iceberg lettuce	
1	head green curly leaf lettuce	
1	medium tomato	
1	carrot sliced 1/16" thick	2 mm.
1	stalk celery sliced 1/16" thick	2 mm.
	Herbal Italian Dressing (bottled)	
	(Add 1 tablespoon olive oil to 2 ozs.	15 ml.
	dressing to improve flavor)	60 ml.

Timetable

6:10 P.M.
Take meat out of refrigerator and leave at room temperature.
6:15
Set Table.
6:30
Prepare ingredients for fruit compote and place in baking dish. Refrigerate until ready for baking.
6:40
Soak broccoli.
6:45
Prepare ingredients for almond butter sauce.
6:50
Prepare broccoli for cooking.
6:55
Prepare potatoes for baking. Preheat oven.
7:00
Prepare ingredients for tournedos creme rouge.
7:10
Place potatoes in oven for baking.
7:15
Prepare salads and refrigerate.
7:30
Puncture the baked potatoes to allow steam to escape.
7:35
Panbroil filets.
7:40
Heat water for broccoli.
7:44
Place heat proof platter for filets in oven with potatoes.
7:45
Place vegetable steamer with broccoli into pan of water and cover.
7:47
Place filets with juice on heated platter and cover on top of stove.
7:48
Start creme rouge sauce.
7:55
Start almond butter sauce.
7:56
Turn off heat under the broccoli.
7:57
Check potatoes and turn off oven if they are done.
7:58
Place broccoli and potatoes in serving bowls, pour sauce over broccoli, pour sauce over the filets and serve with salads and wine.

After dinner finish preparing the fruit compote and serve with tea or coffee.

Preparation:

Tear off a few good leaves of curly lettuce, rinse the leaves and place them on a salad plate. Tear off the outer leaves of the iceberg lettuce from the head. Cut the head into quarters. Tear two of the quarters into bite-sized pieces and pile onto the prepared salad plate. Place the carrots, celery and tomatoes cut into 1/4"/6 mm. wedges in a pleasing arrangement on top of the lettuce.

Drizzle with Italian Dressing just prior to serving.

BROCCOLI AMANDINE

Ingredients:	METRIC
1 lb. broccoli	.5 kg.
1/4 teaspoon salt	1 ml.
1/8 cup chopped salted almonds	15 g.
1 oz. butter (2 tablespoons)	30 g.
1 teaspoon lemon juice	5 ml.

Preparation:

Soak broccoli for 10 minutes in cold water. Drain and remove large leaves and the tough part of the stalks. Cut deep gashes in the bottom of the stalks.

Place one inch of water and 1/4 teaspoon salt in a medium saucepan and bring to a boil over medium high heat.

Place broccoli in a vegetable steamer, put steamer in pan of boiling water, cover and cook over low heat for 10 to 12 minutes.

While broccoli is cooking, place butter in a small saucepan and heat to foaming over medium heat. Add lemon juice and chopped almonds, reduce heat to low and simmer for 3 minutes.

Drain broccoli, place in serving bowl, pour almond butter sauce over broccoli and serve.

BAKED POTATOES

Ingredients:	METRIC
2 large Idaho potatoes	
1 teaspoon butter	5 g.
8 tablespoons sour cream (1/2 cup)	120 ml.
1 tablespoon chopped chives	15 ml.

Preparation:

Wash and scrub potatoes. Dry them and grease them lightly with butter. Bake them in a pre-heated oven at 425°F./220°C. for 40 minutes to 1 hour depending on their size. When the potatoes are 1/2 done, puncture the skin once with a fork to allow the steam to escape. Return them to the oven and finish baking.

Serve with sour cream and chopped chives.

(Potatoes are done when you can easily pierce them over half way through with a fork.)

FRUIT COMPOTE ALA PORT

Ingredients:	METRIC
1/2 jar (8 oz.) dark sweet pitted cherries	225 g.
1/2 can (7 oz.) pineapple chunks	200 g.
1/4 cup Port wine	60 ml.
1/4 cup sour cream	60 ml.
1 teaspoon brown sugar	5 ml.

Preparation:

Place drained cherries in a shallow baking dish or casserole and top with drained pineapple chunks. Drizzle wine over the fruit. Cover and bake in a pre-heated 350°F./175°C. oven for 20 minutes. Stir sour cream until fluffy. Arrange fruit in sherbet glasses, spoon sour cream over each and top with a sprinkling of brown sugar.

Menu

Piquant K-Bobs

Pistachio Rice Salad

Cherries Jubilee

Médoc Wine

Piquant K-Bobs

PIQUANT K-BOBS

Ingredients:		METRIC
1	lb. Sirloin Tip steak cut into 1-1/2" cubes	450 g. / 4 cm.
1	tablespoon butter	15 g.
8	cherry tomatoes	
1/2	jar (1/2lb.) whole boiled onions, drained	225 g.
1	green pepper, cut into 2" squares	5 cm.
1/2	can (1/2lb.) small whole potatoes, drained	225 g.
1/4	lb. whole fresh mushroom caps. Cut stems from whole mushrooms	115 g.
1/2	cup water	120 ml.
1/4	cup soy sauce	60 ml.
1/8	cup brown sugar	20 g.
1/8	cup lemon juice	30 ml.
1/2	small onion, sliced 1/4" thick	6 mm.
1/2	teaspoon minced garlic	2 ml.
1	beef bouillon cube, crushed	

Preparation:

Combine water, soy sauce, sugar, lemon juice, sliced onion, garlic and bouillon cube together in a large bowl. Place meat in bowl, cover and marinate in refrigerator overnight or at least 4 hours. Turn meat several times while it is marinating. Before browning meat let meat stand at room temperature for one hour. Heat butter to foaming in fry pan over medium high heat. Brown meat in heated butter for 4 to 5 minutes turning meat to brown all sides.

Alternate pieces of meat, tomato, onion, green pepper, potato and mushroom on skewers. Brush well with soy marinade and broil about 3 inches/8 cm. from heat for 4 to 5 minutes. Turn and broil other side for 3 to 4 more minutes.

To add a bit of charm, place brandy or flambé soaked cotton on the end of each skewer and ignite when serving.

Timetable **Morning**
Prepare marinade. Place meat
in marinade, cover and
refrigerate until
evening.
7:00 P.M.
Set table.
7:15
Prepare ingredients for
cherries jubilee.
Place cherries and
orange juice in

refrigerator.
7:20
Prepare ingredients for
pistachio rice salad.
Cook rice.
7:30
Prepare ingredients for
piquant k-bobs.
7:45
Brown meat.
7:50
Prepare k-bobs and place

in broiler.
7:55
Prepare vinaigrette
dressing and finish salads.
7:58
Serve salads, k-bobs
and wine.

After dinner prepare
the cherries jubilee
and serve with
tea or coffee.

PISTACHIO RICE SALAD

Ingredients:	METRIC
1/2 cup uncooked long grain rice	115 g.
2 cups water	.5 l.
1/2 teaspoon salt	2 ml.
1/4 cup shelled pistachio nuts	30 g.
1/4 cup currants or raisins	60 g.
VINAIGRETTE DRESSING:	
3 tablespoons vegetable or olive oil	45 ml.
1 tablespoon vinegar	15 ml.
1/4 tablespoon ground cinnamon	4 ml.
1/8 teaspoon salt	.5 ml.
1/8 teaspoon pepper	.5 ml.

Preparation:

Boil water and salt in medium sauce pan over medium high heat. Add rice, cover tightly and cook over low heat for 10 to 12 minutes until rice becomes tender. Drain water from rice and rinse rice thoroughly with hot water. Drain again, turn rice onto a serving platter or dish and leave to dry.

Wisk together all ingredients for the vinaigrette dressing. Mix rice, pistachios and currents, moisten with the dressing and serve.

CHERRIES JUBILEE

Ingredients:	METRIC
1 lb. jar sweet, black pitted cherries	450 g.
1 large orange, rind and juice thereof	
1 tablespoon arrowroot or cornstarch	15 ml.
1 oz. Brandy or flambé	30 ml.
2 scoops vanilla ice cream	
1 tablespoon Grand Marnier	15 ml.

Preparation:

Drain the cherries and place in a small heavy saucepan over medium heat. Add the grated orange rind and strained juice and top with Grand Marnier. Heat until bubbling. Dissolve the arrowroot in 1/4 cup/60 ml. of the reserved cherry juice and add to the cherries, folding the cherries over and over as a thickening sauce forms around them.

Heat the Brandy in a small metal container. Ignite the brandy with a match and pour the flaming liqueur over the cherries at the table.

Place a scoop of vanilla ice cream in each dish and spoon the hot cherries over the ice cream. (If flambé, which can be purchased from a restaurant supply house, is used, it need not be heated prior to igniting.)

Menu

Beef Stroganoff

Mixed Garden Salad

Broccoli in Lemon Butter Sauce

Buttered Noodles

Strawberries Romanoff

Grenache Rosé Wine

Beef Stroganoff

BEEF STROGANOFF

Ingredients:		METRIC
3/4	lb. fillet tenderloin of beef cut	340 g.
	into 1/2" slices	15 mm.
2	small dill pickles diced	
1-1/2	tablespoons butter	25 g.
1	tablespoon minced onion	15 ml.
1/2	lb. sliced mushrooms (about 1	225 g.
	cup sliced mushrooms)	
1/2	teaspoon salt	2 ml.
1/4	teaspoon pepper	1 ml.
1/8	teaspoon nutmeg	.5 ml.
1/2	teaspoon basil	2 ml.
3/4	cup sour cream	175 ml.
1/8	cup dry Sherry	30 ml.

Preparation:

Pound the beef slices with a mallot or the flat side of the large chef's knife until the slices are thin. Cut into strips about 1"/2.5 cm. wide.

In a small frypan, melt 1/2 tablespoon/10 g. butter over medium high heat. When butter foams, add minced onion and sauté for about 30 seconds. Place the beef strips in the pan and sauté for about 1 minute turning strips so they brown evenly on both sides. Lower heat to medium and continue sautéing for 4 to 5 minutes longer. Remove beef strips to a plate and cover them with another plate or lid to keep them warm. Add 1 tablespoon/15 g. butter to the pan and stir until the butter is melted. Add sliced mushrooms and sauté for about 3 minutes over the medium heat. Add the beef and pickle and season with salt, pepper, nutmeg and basil. Lower heat to low and add 1/8 cup/30 ml. dry Sherry and 3/4 cup/175 ml. sour cream. Heat and stir mixture but be careful not to boil. Watch for any sign of bubbles and lower heat if they appear. Heat for about 4 minutes. Pour over noodles and serve.

MIXED GARDEN SALAD

Ingredients:		METRIC
1	head of iceberg lettuce	
1	medium tomato cut into 1/2"	15 mm.
	thick wedges	
1	green pepper sliced 1/8" thick	3 mm.
	Italian dressing (bottled)	

Preparation:

Tear off the outer leaves of the lettuce from the head. Cut the head into quarters. Tear two of the quarters into bite sized pieces. Add the tomato wedges and green pepper. Drizzle with Italian dressing just prior to serving.

BROCCOLI IN LEMON BUTTER SAUCE

Ingredients:		METRIC
1	lb. broccoli	450 g.
1/4	teaspoon salt	1 ml.
1/2	teaspoon lemon-pepper seasoning	2 ml.
2	tablespoons butter	30 g.

Preparation:

Soak broccoli for 10 minutes in cold water. Drain and remove large leaves and tough part of the stalks. Cut deep gashes in the bottom of the stalks.

Place one inch of water in a medium saucepan and bring to a boil over medium high heat. Place broccoli in a vegetable steamer, put steamer in pan of boiling water, cover, cook over low heat for 10 to 13 minutes. Drain, place in serving bowl and cover with lemon butter sauce.

LEMON BUTTER SAUCE PREPARATION:

Heat butter and lemon-pepper seasoning in small sauce pan over low heat for 5 to 6 minutes. Mix well and pour over broccoli.

BUTTERED NOODLES

Ingredients:		METRIC
1/2	lb. medium egg noodles	225 g.
1	teaspoon salt	4 ml.
1	teaspoon vegetable oil	4 ml.

Preparation:

Put 2 qts./2 l. water in a large saucepan, add vegetable oil and salt and bring to a boil over medium high heat. Add noodles and boil for about 6 to 8 minutes. After 6 minutes, check a strand for preferred firmness by tasting. When done, pour into collander placed in sink to drain off water. Put 1 tablespoon/15 g. butter in a serving bowl, cover with the drained noodles and toss until noodles are coated with butter.

STRAWBERRIES ROMANOFF

Ingredients:		METRIC
1	pint box of strawberries	285 g.
1	large orange	
2	tablespoons sugar	30 ml.
1	tablespoon Grand Marnier	15 ml.
1	tablespoon Cognac	15 ml.

Preparation:

Remove stems and wash the strawberries under running cold water. Place the strawberries in a serving dish. Peel the orange and add the orange segments, cutting away the membranes. Squeeze the juice from the remaining orange pulp over the strawberries and orange segments. Sprinkle with sugar. Add Grand Marnier and Cognac. Toss the fruit in the orange juice and combined brandies. Serve immediately. If desired, a tablespoon of Cognac can be gently heated and ignited with a match and poured over the strawberries romanoff when served.

Menu

Beef Bourguignonne Flambé

Spinach Salad

Parsleyed Rice

Simply Cheesecake

Côte de Nuits Wine

Beef Bourguignonne Flambé

BEEF BOURGUIGNONNE FLAMBE

Ingredients:		METRIC
2	slices bacon, cut up into 1" pieces	2.5 cm.
3/4	lb. sirloin tip steak, cut into bite sized strips 1/2" by 1 1/2"	340 g. 15 by 40 mm.
1	tablespoon flour	8 g.
1/2	teaspoon seasoned salt	2 ml.
1/2	cup Burgundy wine	125 ml.
1/2	cup water	125 ml.
1/2	package beef stew seasoning mix	20 g.
6	small boiling onions with ends pierced	
1/8	lb. fresh mushrooms, sliced (about 1/4 cup)	60 g.
6	cherry tomatoes, stems removed	
1/8	cup Brandy or flambé	30 ml.

Preparation:

Fry bacon in a large fry pan over medium high heat until bacon is crisp. Add meat strips that have been coated with flour and seasoned salt. Lower heat to medium and brown the meat carefully for about 5 to 6 minutes, turning the meat to brown all sides. Pour Burgundy and water into pan, sprinkle with beef stew seasoning mix and stir.

Reduce heat to low, cover pan tightly and simmer gently for about 45 minutes.

Add onions and cook for 40 minutes longer.

Add mushrooms and cherry tomatoes and simmer for an additional 5 minutes.

Remove meat to a shallow serving dish. Pour heated Brandy or flambé over top of meat and set aflame at table. Stir gently and serve immediately.

Timetable

Morning
Prepare simply cheesecake and refrigerate.
6:15 P.M.
Prepare ingredients for beef bourguignonne flambé.
6:20
Brown steak strips.
6:27
Simmer steak strips in wine sauce.
6:30
Set table.
6:45
Prepare spinach salad.

7:00
Relax with a glass of wine.
7:12
Add onions to bourguignonne.
7:25
Prepare ingredients for parsleyed rice and start cooking.
7:50
Reduce heat under rice and remove lid.
7:52
Add mushrooms and cherry tomatoes to bourguignonne.
7:56
Heat Brandy.

7:57
Place rice in serving bowl.
7:58
Remove meat to serving dish and place vegetables with sauce in a serving bowl. Set beef aflame with Brandy and serve with rice, vegetables in sauce, salad and wine.

After dinner serve simply cheesecake with tea or coffee.

SPINACH SALAD

Ingredients:	METRIC
1 package fresh spinach, washed and dryed	225 g.
4 medium mushrooms, sliced 1/8" thick	3 mm.
1/8 cup shredded Swiss cheese	15 g.
1/8 cup alfalfa sprouts	30 ml.
French dressing (bottled)	

Preparation:
Tear spinach leaves into bite-sized pieces and place in salad bowls. Add mushrooms, Swiss cheese and alfalfa sprouts and drizzle with French dressing.

PARSLEYED RICE

Ingredients:	METRIC
1 1/3 cup water	300 ml.
1/2 teaspoon salt	2 ml.
1/2 tablespoon butter	8 g.
2 tablespoons chopped fresh parsley	30 ml.
1/2 cup uncooked long grain rice	115 g.

Preparation:
Boil water in medium saucepan over medium high heat. Add salt, butter, parsley and rice. Cover tightly, reduce heat to low and cook for 20 minutes. Uncover and reduce heat to warm for 5 minutes or until all water is absorbed. Fluff rice with fork and serve.

SIMPLY CHEESECAKE

Ingredients:	METRIC
1 8" graham cracker pie shell	20 cm.
2 cups (5oz.) non-dairy whipped topping, thawed	475 ml.
1/4 cup cream Sherry	60 ml.
1/4 cup sugar	50 g.
2 (3oz.) packages cream cheese, softened	170 g.
1 (1lb. 5oz.) can cherry pie filling	600 g.

Preparation:
In a medium bowl beat the Sherry and 1/4 cup/50 g. sugar into the cream cheese. Fold this mixture carefully into the whipped topping and spread into the pie shell. Pour the cherry pie filling over top of the cheese mixture and chill in the refrigerator for at least 4 hours before serving.

Menu

Flank Steak with Herb Stuffing

Cucumber Salad

Potato Parmesan

Crème de Café

St. Emilion Wine

Flank Steak with Herb Stuffing

FLANK STEAK WITH HERB STUFFING

Ingredients:		METRIC
1	lb. flank steak thinly sliced or	450 g.
	pounded 1/8" thick and cut into	3 mm.
	4" wide strips	10 cm.
1	cup herb stuffing mix	85 g.
1/2	teaspoon parsley flakes	2 ml.
1/2	teaspoon Worcestershire sauce	2 ml.
3	tablespoons melted butter	45 g.
2	tablespoons vegetable oil	30 ml.
	wooden toothpicks or cord string	
1	package frozen mixed vegetables in onion sauce	285 g.
1	tablespoon Worcestershire sauce	15 ml.
3	drops Tabasco sauce	3 drops
1/8	teaspoon coarse ground black pepper	.5 ml.

Preparation:

Melt butter in a small saucepan over low heat. Blend stuffing mix, parsley flakes and 1/2 teaspoon/2 ml. Worcestershire sauce into the melted butter until the crumbs are well coated. Spoon the stuffing in equal parts onto the steaks. Roll the steaks with the herb stuffing inside and tie with string or secure with wooden toothpicks.

Heat the vegetable oil in a large fry pan over medium high heat until a drop of water sizzles when dropped into it. Brown the steak rolls on all sides in the vegetable oil for about 4 to 5 minutes.

Transfer the steak rolls to a casserole, cover and bake in a pre-heated 350°F./175°C. oven for about 60 minutes.

Spoon the vegetables in sauce over the meat during the last 15 minutes of baking.

Sauce: Prepare vegetables according to directions on package. Add 1 tablespoon/15 ml. Worcestershire and 3 drops Tabasco, sprinkle with pepper and blend well with a wooden spoon.

Timetable 6:30 P.M.
Prepare cucumber salad and refrigerate.
6:45
Prepare ingredients for flank steak with herb stuffing.
6:49
Pre-heat oven.
6:50
Prepare herb stuffing and roll steaks.
6:55
Brown steaks.
7:00
Place covered casserole in oven to bake.
7:05
Set table.
7:20
Relax with a glass of sherry.
7:30
Rinse cucumbers, arrange on salad plates and refrigerate. Do Not add vinegar dressing.
7:35
Prepare vegetable sauce.
7:40
Heat wine, water, salt and butter for potato parmesan.
7:44
Spoon vegetable sauce over meat in casserole and continue baking.
7:45
Make instant potatoes, prepare casserole and place casserole in oven with flank steak.
7:58
Add vinegar dressing to salad and serve with flank steak, potato parmesan and wine.

After dinner prepare creme de cafe and serve with tea or coffee.

CUCUMBER SALAD

Ingredients:		METRIC
1	medium cucumber sliced 1/8" thick	3 mm.
1/4	teaspoon salt	1 ml.
1/8	teaspoon coarse ground black pepper	.5 ml.
1/2	tablespoon sugar	7 g.
1	tablespoon cider vinegar	15 ml.

Preparation:

Peel cucumber, if preferred. Slice thinly and sprinkle with salt. Place slices on a flat plate, cover with another plate to press the slices and place in refrigerator for 1 hour.

Pour off any liquid that has come off the cucumbers and rinse off excess salt.

Arrange slices on salad plates and add pepper, sugar and vinegar.

POTATO PARMESAN

Ingredients:		METRIC
1/4	cup dry white wine	60 ml.
2/3	cup water	160 ml.
1/4	teaspoon salt	1 ml.
1 1/2	tablespoons butter	23 g.
1/4	cup milk	60 ml.
3/4	cup instant potato buds or 1 cup instant potato flakes	175 ml. or 235 ml.
2	tablespoons parmesan cheese	30 ml.
1	egg yolk, lightly beaten	
1	tablespoon melted butter	15 g.

Preparation:

In a small saucepan combine wine, water, salt and butter and heat to boiling over medium high heat. Remove from heat and add milk, then the instant potatoes, beating until smooth and creamy. Stir in 1 tablespoon/15 ml. of cheese and the egg yolk.

Spoon the potatoes into a small casserole, drizzle with melted butter and sprinkle with the remaining cheese. Bake uncovered in a pre-heated 350°F./175°C. oven for 15 minutes or until lightly browned.

CREME de CAFE

Ingredients:		METRIC
2	large scoops vanilla ice cream	
4	tablespoons coffee liqueur	60 ml.

Preparation:

Place a large scoop of vanilla ice cream in each of two parfait or sherbet glasses and drizzle two tablespoons of coffee liqueur over each.

Menu

Veal in Wine Sauce

Mixed Garden Salad

Tarragon Carrots

Parsleyed Rice

Yogurt Apple Pie

Maconnais Wine

Veal in Wine Sauce

VEAL IN WINE SAUCE

Ingredients:		METRIC
3/4	lb. veal cut from leg	340 g.
2	tablespoons butter	30 g.
2	shallots chopped	
3	mushrooms sliced 1/8" thick	3 mm.
1	teaspoon paprika	4 ml.
1	tablespoon flour	8 g.
3/4	cup white wine	175 ml.
1/4	cup heavy cream	60 ml.
1/8	teaspoon salt	.5 ml.
1/8	teaspoon pepper	.5 ml.
	Parsley for garnish (finely chopped)	

Preparation:

Cut veal into 1"/3 cm. strips. Chop shallots and sauté in foaming butter in medium fry pan over medium high heat until they turn soft and transparent. Add veal strips and sauté over medium high heat for 2 to 3 minutes. Toss in mushrooms and cook for another 2 minutes over medium heat. Stir in paprika and flour and season with salt and pepper. Add the wine to form a medium sauce. Add the cream and cook for 1 more minute.

Garnish with finely chopped parsley and serve on a bed of rice.

Due to the variety of cooking times for veal, taste the veal to determine whether or not is is done before serving.

MIXED GARDEN SALAD

Ingredients:		METRIC
1	head of iceberg lettuce	
1	medium tomato sliced 1/8" thick	3 mm.
1	green pepper sliced 1/8" thick	3 mm.
1/4	cup sliced mushrooms	60 g.
	Sweet & Sour dressing (bottled)	

Timetable 6:30 P.M.
Prepare yogurt apple pie and
pre-heat oven.
7:00
Place pie in oven to bake.
7:02
Set table.
7:17
Prepare salads and refrigerate.
7:27
Prepare ingredients for tarragon
carrots.
7:30
Prepare ingredients for parsleyed

rice and start to cook it.
7:35
Start heating water for carrots.
7:36
Prepare ingredients for veal in
wine sauce.
7:40
Remove pie from oven and cool.
7:41
Place carrots in boiling water,
cover pan and reduce heat.
7:50
Start cooking veal in wine sauce.
7:54

Reduce heat under rice and
remove lid.
7:57
Place carrots in serving bowl.
7:58
Place rice and veal in serving
bowls and serve with carrots,
salads and wine.

After dinner serve the yogurt apple pie with tea or coffee.

Preparation:

Tear off the outer leaves of the lettuce from the head. Cut the head into quarters. Tear two of the quarters into bite sized pieces. Adorn with tomato slices, green pepper and mushrooms.

Drizzle with sweet and sour dressing just prior to serving.

TARRAGON CARROTS

Ingredients:		METRIC
3	medium carrots julienned	
1	tablespoon butter	15 g.
1/2	teaspoon tarragon	2 ml.

Preparation:

Peel the carrots and cut into julienne strips (1/8" thick by 1-1/2"/4 cm. to 2"/5 cm. long).

Place one inch of water into a medium saucepan and bring to a boil over medium high heat. Place carrot strips into the boiling water, cover, reduce heat to low and cook for 15 to 17 minutes.

Drain, sprinkle with tarragon and mix in the butter.

PARSLEYED RICE

Ingredients:		METRIC
1 1/3	cups water	315 ml.
1/2	teaspoon salt	2 ml.
1/2	tablespoon butter	8 g.
2	tablespoons chopped fresh parsley	30 ml.
1/2	cup uncooked long grain rice	115 g.

Preparation:

Boil water in medium saucepan over medium high heat. Add salt, butter, parsley and rice. Cover tightly, reduce heat to low and cook for 20 minutes.

Uncover and reduce heat to warm for 5 minutes or until all water is absorbed. Fluff rice with fork and serve.

YOGURT APPLE PIE

Ingredients:		METRIC
1/2	cup sugar	115 g.
2 1/2	tablespoons all-purpose flour	20 g.
1/2	teaspoon cinnamon	2 ml.
1/8	teaspoon nutmeg	.5 ml.
4	cups peeled and sliced apples (baking variety)	450 g.
1	egg, beaten	
1	cup plain or apple yogurt	225 g.
1/2	teaspoon vanilla extract	2 ml.
1/2	teaspoon almond extract	2 ml.
1	8" pre-made pie shell (9"cut down)	20 cm.
	Topping	
1/4	cup soft butter	55 g.
1/4	cup brown sugar	40 g.
1/4	cup whole-wheat flour	30 g.
2	tablespoons toasted wheat germ	15 g.
1/2	cup chopped walnuts	60 g.

Preparation:

Combine sugar, flour, cinnamon, and nutmeg with apples in a large mixing bowl and set aside. Mix together egg, yogurt, vanilla, and almond extract. Fold yogurt mixture into apples until well blended. Pour into pie shell.

With a pastry blender or spatula crumble butter, sugar, flour and wheat germ until size of peas. Stir in walnuts and spoon mixture over the yogurt-apple mixture.

Bake in a pre-heated 400°F./200°C. oven for 35 to 40 minutes until topping turns medium brown.

Menu

Veal Sinatra

Caesar Salad

Linguini in White Sauce

Lemon Mousse

Médoc Wine

Veal Sinatra

VEAL SINATRA

Ingredients:		METRIC
2	5 oz. veal cutlets pounded very thin (1/8" thick)	140 g. 3 mm.
2	whole eggs beaten	
2	tablespoons grated Romano cheese	15 g.
3	tablespoons butter	45 g.
3	tablespoons vegetable oil	45 ml.
1	cup chicken stock	230 ml.
1/2	cup white wine	120 ml.
1	cup mushrooms, sliced 1/8" thick	240 g. 3 mm.
1/4	cup mozzarella cheese grated	30 g.
1/2	teaspoon granulated garlic	2 ml.
1/2	lemon squeezed for juice	
6	sprigs of fresh watercress	
1/4	cup flour	30 g.

Preparation:

Dredge veal cutlets in flour, then in mixed egg and Romano cheese batter. Heat butter and oil in a fry pan over medium high heat until the foam starts to subside. Saute the veal in the hot butter and oil until brown for about 3 to 4 minutes. Be sure to turn the veal over to brown both sides. Add chicken stock and white wine. Add mushrooms and allow to simmer for 3 minutes at low heat. Top with mozzarella cheese, season with granulated garlic and fresh lemon juice. Cook for 1 or 2 more minutes until cheese melts. Remove the veal to a warm platter, garnish with watercress and serve. Pour the liquid in the pan over the linguini and serve.

Timetable 6:00 P.M.
Prepare the lemon mousse
and refrigerate.
6:15
Set table.
6:30
Relax.
7:00
Prepare ingredients for
Caesar salad and
refrigerate.
7:20
Wrap bread in aluminum
foil.

7:25
Prepare ingredients for
veal Sinatra.
7:42
Heat water for linguini.
7:47
Place linguini in
boiling water.
7:48
Start cooking the
veal Sinatra.
7:50
Pre-heat the oven for the
bread.

7:55
Place bread in oven.
7:57
Drain linguini and place in
serving bowl.
7:58
Place veal in serving platter
and pour liquid over linguini.

Serve veal Sinatra,
linguini, bread and wine and
prepare Caesar salad at table.

CAESAR SALAD

Ingredients:		METRIC
1/2	clove of garlic, minced	
3	tablespoons olive oil	45 ml.
1/4	cup croutons	20 g.
1	head Romaine lettuce	
1/4	teaspoon salt	1 ml.
1/8	teaspoon dry mustard	.5 ml.
1/8	teaspoon fresh ground or coarse ground pepper	.5 ml.
2	anchovy fillets cut into small pieces	
1/2	lemon squeezed for juice	
2	tablespoons Parmesan cheese	15 g.
4	drops Worcestershire sauce	
1	raw egg	
2	tablespoons wine vinegar	30 ml.

Preparation:
Place minced garlic into olive oil and mix. Wash and dry well the Romaine lettuce, separate the leaves and place in a large mixing bowl. Sprinkle the salt, pepper, dry mustard, anchovies and 4 drops of Worcestershire sauce over the Romaine. Add the garlic oil, wine vinegar, and egg to the ingredients of the bowl. Squeeze the juice of 1/2 lemon over the egg in the bowl. Add the croutons and 2 tablespoons/15 g. Parmesan cheese. Toss well and serve immediately.

LINGUINI

Ingredients:		METRIC
1/2	lb. linguini	225 g.
2	teaspoons salt	8 ml.
1	teaspoon vegetable oil	4 ml.
2	oz. Parmesan or Romano cheese	60 g.
2	quarts water	2 l.

Preparation:
Put 2 quarts/2 l. water in a large sauce pan, add vegetable oil and salt and bring to a boil over medium high heat. Add linguini and boil for 9 to 10 minutes at medium heat. After 8 minutes, check a strand of linguini for preferred firmness by tasting. When linguini is done, pour into collander placed in sink to drain off water. *Place 1 tablespoon/15 g. butter in serving bowl, add linguini and mix. Serve with a side dish of Parmesan or Romano cheese.
*(Optional to prevent sticking.)

LEMON MOUSSE

Ingredients:		METRIC
2	egg yolks	
2	tablespoons sugar	30 g.
1	lemon	
1/2	cup whipping cream	120 ml.
1	teaspoon unflavored gelatin	4 ml.

Preparation:
Beat together the egg yolks and sugar until thick. Grate the rind of the lemon and add the grated rind and the juice of the lemon. Place one ounce of water into a small saucepan. Sprinkle gelatin on the water and allow to stand without stirring for three minutes. Melt the gelatin over low heat. Whip the cream lightly. Combine the egg yolk mixture with the cream and gelatin and mix with a hand whip or mixer at the lowest speed. Place in two champagne glasses or parfait glasses and chill for two hours before serving. Top with small peaks of whipped cream and serve.

Menu

Chicken Cordon Bleu

Spinach Salad

Baked Pineapple Rice

Glazed Apples Rosé

Sauvignon Wine

Chicken Cordon Bleu

CHICKEN CORDON BLEU

Ingredients:		METRIC
1	large roaster chicken breast, skinned, boned and halved	
1/8	cup flour	15 g.
1/8	teaspoon salt	.5 ml.
1/8	teaspoon pepper	.5 ml.
1	tablespoon vegetable oil	15 ml.
2	tablespoon butter	30 g.
1/8	cup dry white wine	30 ml.
1/2	cup chicken stock	120 ml.
4	slices prosciutto or ham	
4	slices Swiss or mozzarella cheese	
1	tablespoon melted butter	15 g.
1-1/2	tablespoons bread crumbs	8 g.
4	sprigs fresh parsley	

Preparation:

Cut each breast in half again, lengthwise. Place each piece of chicken between two sheets of wax paper and flatten to one-third inch thickness by pounding with the flat side of a large chef's knife or a meat mallet. Remove the wax paper and trim the cutlets evenly with a sharp knife. Dust each cutlet with flour seasoned with salt and pepper. Heat the oil and 2 tablespoons/20 g. butter in a large fry pan over medium high heat until the butter foam subsides. Brown the cutlets for 2-3 minutes on each side. Remove the cutlets to a heated shallow baking pan. Pour the fat out of the pan and add the wine. Cook the wine over low heat until most of it has evaporated, stirring constantly with a fork. Stir in the stock, increase heat to medium, and whisk the liquid until it boils. Pour this broth into the baking dish with the cutlets. Top each cutlet with a slice of prosciutto or ham and a slice of cheese. Brush with butter and sprinkle lightly with bread crumbs. Place in a pre-heated 375°F./190°C. oven and cook for about 10-12 minutes until the cheese melts and the top is golden.

Garnish with fresh parsley and serve.

Timetable
6:00 P.M.
Cook rice and prepare ingredients for the baked pineapple rice.
6:15
Set table.
6:30
Prepare spinach salads and refrigerate.
6:50
Pre-heat oven.

6:58
Place rice casserole in oven.
7:00
Prepare ingredients for chicken cordon bleu.
7:15
Prepare ingredients for glazed apples Rosé.
7:30
Start to cook the chicken cordon bleu.

7:46
Place cordon bleu in oven and increase oven temperature to 375°F.
7:58
Serve the cordon bleu, salads and wine.

After dinner, prepare the glazed apples Rosé and serve with tea or coffee.

SPINACH SALAD

Ingredients:		METRIC
1	package spinach, washed and dried	225 g.
4	medium mushrooms, sliced 1/8" thick	3 mm.
1/8	cup shredded Swiss cheese	15 g.
1	hard boiled egg, sliced 1/8" thick	3 mm.
	Sweet and Sour Dressing	

Preparation:

Tear spinach leaves into bite sized pieces and place in salad bowls. Add mushrooms, Swiss cheese and egg slices. Drizzle with Sweet and Sour Dressing before serving.

BAKED PINEAPPLE RICE

Ingredients:		METRIC
1/2	cup uncooked long grain white rice	115 g.
1-1/3	cups water	315 ml.
1/4	teaspoon salt	1 ml.
1/2	tablespoon butter	8 g.
1-1/2	cups cubed pineapple	225 g.
3	tablespoons butter	45 g.
1/2	cup brown sugar	8 g.
1/4	cup pineapple juice	60 ml.

Preparation:

Boil water, salt, and 1/2 tablespoon/8 g. butter in a medium sauce pan over medium high heat. Add the rice, cover tightly and cook over low heat for 20 minutes.

Uncover and reduce heat to warm for 5 minutes or until all the water is absorbed. Drain the pineapple and cut into small pieces. Place in a small buttered casserole or individual baking cups 1/3 the rice and dot with 1 tablespoon/15 g. butter. Cover with 1/2 the pineapple and sprinkle with 1/4 cup/4 g. brown sugar. Repeat the layer of rice dotted with butter and add the remaining pineapple sprinkled with 1/4 cup/4 g. brown sugar. Place the last 1/3 rice on top, dot with butter, cover, and bake in a pre-heated 350°F./175°C. oven for 1 hour.

GLAZED APPLES ROSÉ

Ingredients:		METRIC
2	cooking apples	
1/4	cup Rosé wine	60 ml.
1/2	tablespoon lemon juice	8 ml.
1/4	cup sugar	60 g.
1/8	teaspoon cinnamon	.5 ml.
1/8	teaspoon nutmeg	.5 ml.
1/16	teaspoon salt	.2 ml.
1	tablespoon orange marmalade	15 g.
2	scoops vanilla ice cream	

Preparation:

Peel, quarter, and remove the cores from the apples. Combine the wine, lemon juice, sugar, spices and salt in a small sauce pan and heat over low heat to simmering. Add the apples, cover and cook gently until tender, about 20 minutes. Remove the apples, add marmalade to the liquid remaining in the pan and heat over low heat, stirring until the marmalade is melted. Place the apples in small bowls, spoon the sauce over the apples and serve with a scoop of vanilla ice cream.

Menu

Breast of Chicken Piccante

Country Salad

Glazed Carrots

Parsleyed Rice

Banana Cream Crunch

Chablis Wine

Breast of Chicken Piccante

BREAST OF
CHICKEN PICCANTE

Ingredients:		METRIC
2	boneless, skinned chicken breasts, split and pounded thin, 1/8"	3 mm.
1/2	lemon, sliced 1/8"	3 mm.
2/3	cup white wine	160 ml.
1/8	cup lemon juice	30 ml.
4	tablespoons flour, to flour chicken breasts	30 g.
1/2	tablespoon instant flour to thicken sauce	4 g.
2	tablespoons butter	30 g.
4	mushrooms, sliced 1/8"	3 mm.

Preparation:

Put flour in paper bag, add the towel dried chicken breasts, close bag tightly, and shake to coat the breasts with flour. Heat the butter in a fry pan over medium heat until the butter foam starts to subside. Place the floured chicken breasts in the pan and saute for 3-4 minutes on each side until they are medium brown. Place the chicken breasts in a heated oven-proof platter and keep warm in a 250°F./120°C. oven. Add the wine and mushrooms to the heated butter, deglaze the pan and cook over medium heat for 1 minute. Add the lemon juice and cook for about 5 minutes until the liquid decreases to half its volume. Add 1/2 tablespoon/4 g. instant flour very slowly while stirring consantly until the sauce thickens. Pour the sauce over the chicken breasts, garnish with the lemon slices, and serve over a bed of rice.

Morning
Prepare banana cream crunch and refrigerate.
6:30 P.M.
Prepare salads and refrigerate.
6:45
Set table.
7:00
Prepare ingredients for chicken piccante.
7:15
Prepare ingredients for glazed carrots.
7:30
Prepare ingredients for parsleyed rice and start cooking it.
7:35
Start cooking the glazed carrots.
7:40
Start cooking the chicken piccante.
7:48
Start the sauce for the chicken piccante.
7:52
Uncover rice and reduce heat to warm.
7:53
Drain the carrots, add butter, sugar, and cinnamon and simmer until well glazed.
7:58
Place rice and carrots in serving bowls. Pour sauce over the chicken breasts, garnish, and serve with rice, carrots, salads, and wine.

After dinner serve the banana cream crunch with tea or coffee.

COUNTRY SALAD

Ingredients:		METRIC
1	head iceberg lettuce	
1/4	lb. fresh green beans, washed with ends clipped	110 g.
1/8	cup alfalfa sprouts	30 ml.
1/8	cup shredded carrots	30 ml.
2	tablespoons slivered almonds	15 g.
	Herbal Italian Dressing	

Preparation:
Tear off the outer leaves of the lettuce from the head. Cut the head into quarters. Tear two of the quarters into bite sized pieces. Add the fresh green beans cut in half, shredded carrots, alfalfa sprouts and slivered almonds. Drizzle with Italian Dressing just prior to serving.

GLAZED CARROTS

Ingredients:		METRIC
4	medium carrots, julienned	
1	tablespoon butter	15 g.
1	tablespoon sugar or honey	15 g.
1/2	teaspoon cinnamon	2 ml.

Preparation:
Peel the carrots and cut into julienne strips (1/8-1/4 inch/3 mm.-6 mm. thick by 1-1/2 to 2 inches/4 cm.-5 cm. long).

Place one inch of water in a medium sauce pan and bring to a boil over medium high heat. Place the carrot strips into the boiling water, cover, reduce the heat to low and cook for 15-17 minutes. Drain the liquid and add the butter, sugar and cinnamon. Simmer the carrots in this mixture over low heat until well glazed.

PARSLEYED RICE

Ingredients:		METRIC
1-1/3	cups water	315 ml.
1/2	teaspoon salt	2 ml.
1/2	tablespoon butter	8 g.
2	tablespoons chopped fresh parsley	30 ml.
1/2	cup uncooked, long grain white rice	115 g.

Preparation:
Boil the water in a medium sauce pan over medium high heat. Add salt, butter, parsley and rice. Cover tightly and reduce the heat to low. Cook for 20 minutes. Uncover and reduce the heat to warm for 5 minutes or until all the water is absorbed. Fluff with a fork and serve.

BANANA CREAM CRUNCH

Ingredients:		METRIC
1	8 inch graham cracker pie shell (pre-made)	20 cm.
1	3-3/4 oz. package instant vanilla pudding	110 g.
1-1/2	cups milk	350 ml.
1/4	cup dry or medium Sherry	60 ml.
1/2	cup heavy cream	120 ml.
2	small bananas, sliced 1/8" thick	3 mm.
1/8	teaspoon nutmeg	.5 ml.

Preparation:
Combine the instant pudding mix and milk. Beat with a whisk or rotary beater until the mixture thickens, about 1 to 2 minutes. Stir in the Sherry and let stand a few minutes until set. Whip the cream with the whisk or beater until stiff and fold into the pudding. Spoon half of the pudding mixture into the pie shell. Top with sliced bananas, cover with the remaining pudding, sprinkle with nutmeg and refrigerate for at least 4 hours.

Menu

Paprika Chicken

Green Salad Supreme

Ratatouille

Buttered Noodles

Strawberries Michèle

Brittany Wine

Paprika Chicken

PAPRIKA CHICKEN

Ingredients:		METRIC
2	tablespoons butter	30 g.
1	tablespoon vegetable oil	15 ml.
1	lb. deboned chicken breasts	450 g.
1/8	teaspoon salt	.5 ml.
1/8	teaspoon pepper	.5 ml.
1	tablespoon paprika	30 g.
1/8	cup finely chopped onion	20 g.
1/4	cup dry white wine	60 ml.
1/2	cup sour cream	120 ml.
2	sprigs fresh parsley	

Preparation:

In a large fry pan melt butter in oil over medium high heat until butter foam subsides. Add chicken pieces and brown gently, 2 or 3 minutes per side. Season with salt and pepper, sprinkle with paprika and turn chicken well to coat all pieces. Add onions and wine. Reduce heat to low, cover pan and cook for 20 minutes or until the chicken is tender when pricked with a fork. While cooking chicken occasionally turn the pieces and baste with the liquid. Remove the chicken to a hot serving platter. Blend the cream into the liquid and heat for about 3 minutes, stirring continuously. Pour the sauce over the chicken and serve over a bed of noodles with a garnish of fresh parsley.

GREEN SALAD SUPREME

Ingredients:		METRIC
1	package spinach, washed and dried	225 g.
1/4	head of iceberg lettuce	
1/2	cup raw broccoli, washed and broken into bite-sized bits	115 g.
1/4	cup alfalfa sprouts	60 ml.
	Spicy Italian Dressing	

Preparation:

Break spinach and lettuce into bite-sized pieces. Add the broccoli and alfalfa sprouts and drizzle just prior to serving.

Timetable **6:15 P.M.**
Prepare salads and refrigerate. Cut eggplant and sprinkle with salt.
6:30
Set table.
6:45
Prepare ingredients for strawberries Michele and refrigerate.
6:55
Prepare ingredients for paprika chicken.
7:10
Prepare ingredients for ratatouille and start to cook.
7:28

Start cooking the paprika chicken while the ratatouille is simmering.
7:35
Cover pan and start to simmer the paprika chicken.
7:45
Start heating water for noodles.
7:50
Place noodles in boiling water.
7:54
Cover and reduce heat under the ratatouille.
7:55
Remove chicken to hot serving plate and

prepare sauce.
7:57
Remove bay leaf from the ratatouille, place in serving bowl and garnish.
7:58
Drain noodles and place in serving bowl.
7:59
Pour sauce over chicken and serve with noodles, ratatouille, salads and wine.

After dinner prepare the strawberries Michele and serve with tea or coffee.

BUTTERED NOODLES

Ingredients:		METRIC
1/2	lb. noodles	225 g.
1	teaspoon salt	4 ml.
1	teaspoon vegetable oil	5 ml.
2	oz. parmesan or romano cheese	60 g.
2	tablespoons butter	30 g.

Preparation:

Place 2 quarts/2 l. of water in a large sauce pan, add vegetable oil and salt and bring to a boil over medium high heat. Add the noodles and boil for 6 to 8 minutes. After 6 minutes, check a strand of noodle for preferred firmness by tasting. When noodles are done, pour into the collander placed in the sink to drain off the water. Put 2 tablespoons/30 g. butter in a warm serving bowl, cover with the drained noodles and toss until the noodles are coated with the butter. Serve with a side dish of parmesan or romano cheese.

RATATOUILLE

Ingredients:		METRIC
1/4	medium eggplant cut into 1/2" thick slices, then into 1" chunks	10 mm. 25 mm.
1/4	tablespoon salt	3 ml.
1/8	cup olive oil	30 ml.
1/2	large onion, sliced 1/8"	3 mm.
1	clove garlic, crushed	
1/2	medium green pepper, cored and cut into cubes	
1	medium zucchini sliced 1/4" thick	6 mm.
1	medium tomato, blanched, peeled and cut into 1" cubes	25 mm.
1/8	teaspoon salt	.5 ml.
1/8	teaspoon course ground pepper	.5 ml.
1/8	teaspoon thyme	.5 ml.
1/8	teaspoon oregano	.5 ml.
1	bayleaf	
1	tablespoon chopped parsley	15 ml.

Preparation:

After cutting the eggplant, sprinkle with 1/4 tablespoon/ 3 ml. salt, let stand for 30 minutes, then dry thoroughly. Heat oil in a large fry pan over medium high heat. Sauté onions and garlic for 2 minutes. Add peppers and cook for 2 minutes at medium heat. Add eggplant, brown on both sides for 3 minutes. Add zucchini, tomatoes, and seasonings, except parsley. Simmer uncovered over low heat for 30 minutes. Baste often. Cover and reduce heat to warm for 3 minutes. Remove bay leaf, garnish with fresh parsley and serve.

STRAWBERRIES MICHELE

Ingredients:		METRIC
1/2	cup sour cream	120 ml.
1/2	cup heavy cream	120 ml.
2	tablespoons sugar	30 g.
1/2	lemon, juiced	
3	tablespoons kirschwasser	45 ml.
10	strawberries cut into halves	

Preparation:

Whisk together sour cream and heavy cream with sugar. Add kirsch and 14 strawberry halves. Mix gently and place in wine goblets with 3 half strawberries on top of each dessert.

Menu

Coq Au Vin

Tomatoes Gervais

Rum Peaches

Pinot Chardonnay Wine

Coq Au Vin

COQ AU VIN

Ingredients:		METRIC
2	chicken breasts	
2	chicken legs or thighs	
1/4	cup flour	30 g.
4	carrots chopped into 1/2" pieces	12 mm.
2	medium potatoes peeled and quartered	
2	medium onions peeled and quartered	
8	mushrooms halved	
2	tablespoons vegetable oil	30 ml.
1/2	teaspoon basil	2 ml.
1/2	teaspoon tarragon	2 ml.
1/2	teaspoon white pepper	2 ml.
1/2	teaspoon salt	2 ml.
1/2	cup white wine	125 ml.
1/2	cup chicken stock	125 ml.
1	clove garlic skinned and minced	

Preparation:

Place flour, salt, and pepper in a medium sized plastic or paper bag. Place the chicken pieces towel dried in the bag, one piece at a time and shake the bag until the pieces are covered with flour. Heat oil in a medium fry pan over medium high heat until a drop of water placed into the oil sizzles. Brown the chicken pieces on both sides, about 3 minutes per side. Add the onion and garlic and continue browning for 1 more minute. Add the chicken stock and wine. Lower the heat to low. Add the potatoes, mushrooms, carrots and seasonings. Cover and simmer at very low heat for 50 minutes to 1 hour. After 40 minutes check to see if enough liquid is left in the pan. If liquid has evaporated, add 1/4 cup/60 ml. more white wine and finish cooking.

TOMATOES GERVAIS

Ingredients:		METRIC
2	large tomatoes	
1/8	teaspoon salt	.5 ml.
1/8	teaspoon pepper	.5 ml.
1	package (3 oz.) cream cheese	85 g.
2	tablespoons light cream	30 ml.
1	tablespoon chopped chives	15 ml.
1/4	cup vinaigrette dressing	60 ml.
1	bunch watercress	

Ingredients for vinaigrette:		
1	tablespoon wine vinegar	15 ml.
3	tablespoons olive oil	45 ml.
1/16	teaspoon salt	1 pinch
1/16	teaspoon pepper	1 pinch
1/8	teaspoon marjoram	.5 ml.
1/8	teaspoon basil	.5 ml.
1/8	teaspoon thyme	.5 ml.

Preparation:

Peel the tomatoes by plunging them in a sauce pan of boiling water for 10 seconds. Drain the boiling water and cover the tomatoes with cold water. The skins can then be carefully removed with a paring knife. Cut a slice from the bottom (not stalk end) of each tomato, reserving the slices. Holding the tomato in the palm of your hand, scoop out the seeds with the handle of a teaspoon, using the bowl of the spoon to detach the core. Drain the seeded tomatoes and season the insides lightly with salt and pepper. Soften the cream cheese by mashing with a wooden spoon in a small bowl. Add the light cream and mix until the cheese attains a smooth light texture. A wire whisk or an electric mixer can be used. Season with salt and pepper and add half of the chives. With a teaspoon, fill the tomatoes with the cheese mixture, piling it up well. Spoon on a little of the vinaigrette dressing, reserving the rest to be added just before serving. Cover the tomatoes and chill for up to 2 hours. Just before serving, garnish with watercress and sprinkle with the remaining vinaigrette dressing and chives.

RUM PEACHES

Ingredients:		METRIC
1	can (1 lb.) of peaches (halves)	450 g.
2	tablespoons almonds, chopped	7 g.
4	cookies crumbled (Pepperidge Farm Bordeaux type)	
2	teaspoons sugar	10 g.
2	tablespoons dark Jamaican rum	30 ml.
1/2	cup whipping cream	120 ml.

Preparation:

Drain the peaches, reserving the juice. Place peach halves, cavity side up, in a baking dish or individual baking cups. Combine nuts, sugar, cookies and rum, and place a little of the mixture in each peach cavity. Put one quarter cup of the drained peach juice around the peaches and bake for 30 minutes in a pre-heated oven at 250°F./120°C. Serve hot, topped with whipped cream.

Menu

Brandied Chicken Breasts

Spinach Salad

Tomatoes Au Gratin

Wild and Nutty Rice

Pineapple Delight

Bernkastel Wine

Brandied Chicken Breasts

BRANDIED CHICKEN BREASTS

Ingredients:		METRIC
2	medium boned and skinned chicken breasts	
1/8	cup Brandy	30 ml.
3	tablespoons butter	45 g.
1/8	teaspoon salt	.5 ml.
1/8	teaspoon pepper	.5 ml.
1/8	teaspoon marjoram	.5 ml.
1/4	cup dry sherry	60 ml.
1	cup light cream	235 ml.
2	egg yolks	
1/8	teaspoon salt	.5 ml.
1/8	teaspoon pepper	.5 ml.
1/8	teaspoon nutmeg	.5 ml.
1/8	cup grated Swiss cheese	15 g.
1/8	cup fine buttered bread crumbs	10 g.

Preparation:

Rub chicken breasts with Brandy and let them set for about 10 minutes. Season the chicken breasts with salt, pepper and marjoram.

Heat butter in a fry pan over medium heat until butter foam subsides. Sauté the breasts for 6 to 8 minutes on each side. Remove the breasts to a heated ovenproof platter and keep them warm in a 250°F./120°C. oven.

To the remaining butter in the pan, add the sherry and simmer over low heat until the liquid is reduced to half, about 3 minutes. Add, stirring constantly, the cream which you should first beat with the egg yolks and season with salt, pepper, and nutmeg. Stir and cook until the sauce thickens slightly, about 3 minutes. Pour the sauce over the chicken breasts. Sprinkle with Swiss cheese and crumbs and glaze under the broiler for about 2 minutes until the cheese melts and turns a golden brown.

Timetable

6:15 P.M.
Prepare ingredients for pineapple delight and refrigerate.
6:30
Set table.
6:45
Prepare spinach salads and refrigerate.
7:00
Prepare ingredients for brandied chicken breasts, rub chicken in brandy and set aside.
7:15
Prepare ingredients for tomatoes au gratin.
7:30
Prepare ingredients for wild and nutty rice and start cooking.

7:33
Start sauteing the chicken breasts.
7:38
Pre-heat the oven for the tomatoes.
7:40
Place the tomatoes into the oven and bake.
7:48
Remove chicken breasts to a heated platter and cover to keep warm.
7:49
Start sauce for chicken.
7:53
Uncover rice and reduce heat to warm.

7:55
Remove tomatoes from oven and cover to keep warm.
7:56
Place chicken in broiler to melt cheese.
7:57
Place rice in serving bowl, fluff and sprinkle with walnuts.
7:58
Place tomatoes in serving bowl and serve with rice, chicken, salads and wine.

After dinner prepare pineapple delight and serve with tea or coffee.

SPINACH SALAD

Ingredient:		METRIC
1	package spinach, washed and dried	225 g.
1	hard boiled egg, sliced	
2	tablespoons crumbled bacon or bacon bits	30 ml.
	Bleu cheese dressing (bottled)	

Preparation:

Break the spinach leaves into bite-sized pieces, place on salad plates, add the hard boiled egg slices and bacon bits and drizzle with bleu cheese dressing prior to serving.

TOMATOES AU GRATIN

Ingredients:		METRIC
2	firm large tomatoes	
2	tablespoons brown sugar	10 g.
1/2	teaspoon seasoned salt	2 ml.
1	tablespoon butter	15 g.
2	tablespoons parmesan cheese	15 g.
2	tablespoons seasoned bread crumbs	10 g.

Preparation:

Cut 1"/25 mm. diameter deep holes in each tomato, cutting out the core. Push half of the brown sugar, seasoned salt and butter into the hollows of each tomato. Mix the parmesan cheese and bread crumbs and fill the remaining space with this mixture. Place a small dot of butter on top of each tomato and place the tomatoes in a greased casserole. Bake the casserole, uncovered, for about 15 minutes in a pre-heated 400°F./200°C. oven.

WILD AND NUTTY RICE

Ingredients:		METRIC
1/2	package (3oz.) long grain and wild rice mix	85 g.
1	tablespoon butter	15 g.
1	cup water	235 ml.
1/4	cup rosé wine	60 ml.
1/4	teaspoon salt	1 ml.
1/4	cup coarsley chopped walnuts	15 g.

Preparation:

Prepare the rice according to the package directions, using the 1 cup/235 ml. water and 1/4 cup/60 ml. wine as the liquid. When the rice is finished, place in a serving bowl, fluff rice, sprinkle walnuts on top of rice and serve.

PINEAPPLE DELIGHT

Ingredients:		METRIC
1	fresh pineapple	
2	scoops lemon ice	
2	tablespoons crème de menthe	30 ml.
1	tablespoon sugar	15 g.

Preparation:

Cut off the top of the pineapple. Cut the pineapple into quarters by first cutting along its length then along its width. Slice out the pineapple meat by cutting 1/4"/ 6 mm. from the outside skin. Cut out the tough center core. Cut the fruit into bite-sized pieces and place them in a small bowl. Mix the sugar into the fruit and place the fruit and shells into the refrigerator to chill. When ready to serve, place the fruit into two shell quarters, add a scoop of lemon ice to each and drizzle with crème de menthe. The plume-like stalk of the pineapple can be used as garnish.

Menu

Scallops in Wine Sauce

Tomato Herbal Salad

Spinach Pie Ala Lilly

Fruit with Honey Sauce

Brittany Wine

Scallops in Wine Sauce

SCALLOPS IN WINE SAUCE

Ingredients:		METRIC
1/3	cup Sauternes wine	85 ml.
3/4	lb. fresh or frozen scallops, thawed and drained	340 g.
1 1/2	tablespoons butter	25 g.
1	green onion, chopped	
1/4	cup canned, drained mushrooms (slices)	60 g.
1/4	tablespoon chopped parsley or parsley flakes	3. ml.
1/16	teaspoon salt	1 pinch
1/16	teaspoon pepper	1 pinch
1/16	teaspoon marjoram	1 pinch
1/16	teaspoon thyme	1 pinch
2	teaspoons flour (instant)	5 g.
1/4	cup undiluted evaporated milk	60 ml.
1/4	teaspoon paprika	1 ml.
1/8	cup breadcrumbs	10 g.
2	teaspoons butter	5 g.

Preparation:

In a medium sauce pan heat the wine, add scallops and simmer for about 3 minutes over medium heat. Drain the cooked scallops (saving the liquid) and keep scallops warm in a covered baking dish.

In another sauce pan melt butter over medium heat, add onions and cook until the onions turn light brown. Add the mushrooms, parsley, salt, pepper, marjoram and thyme. Remove from heat and blend in instant flour gradually, stirring constantly. Slowly stir in the evaporated milk and 1/4 cup/60 ml. of the liquid from the scallops. Place pan over medium heat and heat to boiling, stirring constantly. When sauce thickens, add paprika and scallops and remove from heat.

Fill individual baking dishes with the mixture, sprinkle with bread crumbs and dot with butter. Place under broiler until slightly browned and serve.

TOMATO HERBAL SALAD

Ingredients:		METRIC
2	medium tomatoes, sliced 1/4" thick	6 mm.
1/8	teaspoon salt	.5 ml.
1/2	tablespoon olive oil	8 ml.
1	tablespoon wine vinegar	15 ml.
1/8	teaspoon chopped parsley	.5 ml.
1/8	teaspoon chopped chives	.5 ml.
1/8	teaspoon chopped basil	.5 ml.

Timetable 6:00 P.M.
Set table.
6:15
Prepare salads and refrigerate.
6:30
Prepare ingredients for spinach pie a la Lilly.
6:45
Prepare ingredients for fruit with honey sauce.
6:55
Start to cook spinach.
7:10
Saute onion and garlic for spinach pie.
7:13
Pre-heat oven.

7:14
Add spinach to onion and cook.
7:18
Place spinach pie into oven and bake.
7:28
Reduce oven heat for spinach pie.
7:29
Prepare ingredients for scallops in wine sauce.
7:45
Start to cook scallops.
7:50
Saute onions for scallops.
7:56
Remove spinach pie from oven

and broil scallops until slightly browned.
7:58
Serve salads, spinach pie, scallops and wine.
8:00
Place fruit with honey sauce into oven to bake.
8:30
Add bananas.
8:35
Turn off oven.

After dinner place fruit with honey sauce into serving bowls or snifters, garnish and serve with tea or coffee.

Preparation:

Arrange the tomato slices on salad plates. Sprinkle with salt, olive oil, and wine vinegar. Top with a sprinkling of herbs and refrigerate for 1 hour before serving.

SPINACH PIE ALA LILLY

Ingredients:		METRIC
2	pre-made pie shells, (8" or 9" cut down)	20 cm.
1/2	teaspoon salt	2 ml.
2	packages spinach (20 oz.)	565 g.
1	medium onion, sliced 1/8" thick	3 mm.
2	cloves garlic, minced	
4	tablespoons butter	60 g.
1	cup grated mozzarella cheese	115 g.
7	eggs	
1	teaspoon sugar	5 g.

Preparation:

Cut the stems from the spinach and wash several times to remove all sand and soil. Place two cups water and salt into a medium sauce pan and bring to a boil over medium high heat. Place the spinach into the boiling water, cover, reduce heat to low and simmer for about 10 minutes. Drain the water from the spinach.

Place 4 tablespoons butter in fry pan and heat to bubbling over medium high heat. Add the onion and garlic and saute until the onion starts to lightly brown. Add the spinach, lower the heat to low and cook for 3 minutes while stirring the spinach constantly. Mix 2 eggs with the grated mozzarella. Move the fry pan to an unheated burner and add the cheese mixture to the spinach. Mix gently and put the mixture into an 8"/20 cm. pie tin lined with the prepared pie shell. Make 4 holes in

the spinach mixture with an egg as a form. Break 4 eggs without breaking the yolks and place one raw egg into each hole. Cover the pie with the second pie shell.

Mix one egg yolk (carefully separate the yolk from the white by slowly pouring the egg white from one cup to another leaving the yolk in the original cup) with sugar and paint the mixture on the top pie shell with a pastry brush or small paint brush. Prick the top shell in a few places with a fork and bake in a pre-heated oven at 425°F./220°C. for 10 minutes then lower the heat to 300°F./150°C. and bake for about 30 more minutes until the crust turns a golden brown.

FRUIT WITH HONEY SAUCE

Ingredients:		METRIC
1	peach, peeled and cubed	
1	cup pineapple chunks, drained	150 g.
1	apple, peeled, cored and cut into rings	
1/2	cup pineapple juice	120 ml.
1/4	cup honey	60 g.
1	thin lemon slice	
1	stick cinnamon	
1	banana, sliced lengthwise and then in half	
1/2	cup whipped cream	120 ml.
2	cherries or grapes	
1	tablespoon sliced almonds	7 g.

Preparation:

Combine all ingredients except last 4 in a casserole. Cover and bake at 350°F./175°C. for 30 minutes, add banana and bake 5 more minutes. Spoon into serving bowls, garnish with whipped cream and cherries and serve.

Menu

Shrimp Sarapico

Orange/Cucumber Salad

Green Beans Amandine

Sauternes Rice

Strawberry Champagne Sherbet

Grenache Rosé Wine

Shrimp Sarapico

SHRIMP SARAPICO

Ingredients:		METRIC
3/4	lb. fresh or frozen large shrimp, uncooked	340 g.
1	(3oz.) package cream cheese	85 g.
1	(3oz.) package bleu cheese	85 g.
2	pimientos, chopped fine	
4	thin slices lemon	
1/8	cup dry white wine	30 ml.

Preparation:

Shell, clean, devane and wash shrimp. Cream together cheese and pimientos. Cut two squares of aluminum foil, 12"/30 cm. by 12"/30 cm. On each square, mound an equal amount of cheese mixture. Flatten cheese mounds slightly with the back of a spoon. Divide the raw shrimp, placing equal amounts on each cheese mound. Top each with two lemon slices. Bring the edges of foil up to form a bag. Pour 1 tablespoon/15 ml. wine in each bag and seal. Bake in a pre-heated oven at 350°F./175°C. for 25 minutes. (Be sure to place foil bags on a baking sheet or in a broiler pan when baking to avoid spillage.)

Timetable 6:30 P.M.
Set table.
6:45
Prepare salads and refrigerate.
7:00
Prepare ingredients for shrimp sarapico.
7:15
Prepare ingredients for green beans amandine.
7:28
Pre-heat oven.
7:30
Start cooking rice.

7:33
Place shrimp in oven to bake.
7:35
Start cooking the green beans.
7:40
Relax with a glass of wine.
7:52
Uncover the rice and reduce heat.
7:53
Start cooking the amandine sauce.
7:58
Place rice, shrimp and green

beans in serving bowls. Cover beans with sauce and serve with salads, rice, shrimp and wine.

After dinner prepare the strawberry Champagne sherbet and serve with tea or coffee.

ORANGE/CUCUMBER SALAD

Ingredients:		METRIC
1	medium orange, peeled and sliced 1/4" thick (Remove seeds)	6 mm.
1	medium cucumber, washed and sliced 1/4" thick	6 mm.
	Green goddess or creamy Italian salad dressing (bottled)	

Preparation:

Arrange orange slices and cucumber slices on salad plates. Drizzle with dressing just prior to serving.

GREEN BEANS AMANDINE

Ingredients:		METRIC
8	oz. fresh green beans (frozen green beans can be substituted. Follow the instructions for cooking on the package.)	225 g.
1	whole onion, peeled	
1/8	cup butter	30 g.
1/8	cup blanched, shredded almonds	15 g.
1/8	teaspoon salt	.5 ml.

Preparation:

Wash the green beans, snip off the ends and cut each bean in half using a diagonal cut. Place one inch of water in a medium sauce pan and bring to a boil over medium high heat. Place the cut green beans and onion into a vegetable steamer, put the steamer into the pan of boiling water, cover and cook over low heat for about 15 minutes.

Drain off the water, place into a serving bowl and cover with amandine sauce.

Sauce: melt butter in a small sauce pan over low heat. Add almonds and sauté until lightly browned. Sprinkle with salt and pour over green beans.

SAUTERNES RICE

Ingredients:		METRIC
1/2	cup Sauternes wine	125 ml.
3/4	cup water	185 ml.
1/2	teaspoon seasoned salt	2 ml.
1/2	cup uncooked long grain white rice	115 g.
1/8	cup chopped salted peanuts	15 g.
1	tablespoon butter	15 g.
1/4	teaspoon grated orange peel	1 ml.

Preparation:

Boil water, wine and salt in a medium sauce pan over medium high heat. Add rice, cover tightly and cook over low heat for 20 minutes. Uncover and reduce heat to warm for 5 minutes or until all water is absorbed. Remove from heat and stir very lightly into the rice the chopped peanuts, butter and orange peel and serve.

STRAWBERRY CHAMPAGNE SHERBET

Ingredients:	
2	large scoops strawberry sherbet
1	split of Champagne
2	large strawberries

Preparation:

Place a large scoop of sherbet in each of two snifters or Champagne glasses. Pour well chilled Champagne over the sherbet, garnish with strawberries and serve.

Menu

Flounder Végétal

Nutty Apple Grape Salad

Sherried Orange Rice

Amaretto Delight

Côte de Beaune Wine

Flounder Vegetal

FLOUNDER VEGETAL

Ingredients:		METRIC
3/4	lb. flounder fillets	340 g.
2	stalks celery sliced 1/4" thick	6 mm.
1	carrot, peeled and sliced 1/4" thick	6 mm.
1/4	lb. mushrooms sliced 1/4" thick (1/2 cup)	115 g.
1	medium zucchini sliced 1/4" thick and then cut slices in half	6 mm.
1	cup broccoli pieces	230 g.
3	tablespoons butter	45 g.
1/3	cup dry white wine	85 ml.
4	parsley sprigs	
1/2	small onion chopped	

Preparation:

Melt 3 tablespoons/45 g. butter in a large fry pan over medium high heat. When butter foam starts to subside, sauté celery, onion, carrot, mushrooms, zucchini and broccoli for 3 to 4 minutes. Pour 1/3 cup/85 ml. wine over vegetables, reduce heat to low and simmer for 2 minutes. Place vegetables and wine in casserole.

Roll flounder fillets (skin side in) and hold in place with toothpicks. Place the fillets on top of the vegetables and cover the casserole. Place the casserole in a pre-heated 350°F./175°C. oven and bake for 15 to 20 minutes until the fillets become flaky. Place parsley sprigs around the fish and serve over a bed of rice.

Timetable 6:30 P.M.
Set table.
6:45
Prepare salads and refrigerate.
7:00
Prepare ingredients for sherried orange rice.
7:03
Pre-heat oven.
7:04
Boil chicken broth, orange juice and Sherry.

7:08
Place rice mixture into oven and bake.
7:10
Prepare ingredients for flounder vegetal.
7:32
Sauté vegetables for flounder vegetal.
7:38
Place flounder in oven and bake.

7:53
Take rice out of oven.
7:58
Take flounder out of oven and serve with rice, salads and wine.

After dinner prepare the Amaretto delight and serve with tea or coffee.

NUTTY APPLE GRAPE SALAD

Ingredients:		METRIC
1	medium tart apple, peeled, quartered and cored	
1/4	lb. blue grapes, halved and seeded	115 g.
1/4	cup shelled walnuts	30 g.
1	stalk garden mint (leaves only)	
2	teaspoons sugar	10 g.
1	tablespoon lemon juice	15 ml.
1	tablespoon Brandy	15 ml.
1	head bibb lettuce	

Preparation:

Cut the apples crosswise in 1/8'' slices. Place apples, grapes and mint leaves in a bowl. Sprinkle with sugar, lemon juice and Brandy. Toss lightly, arrange on bibb lettuce leaves on salad plates, top with walnuts and chill in the refrigerator for 1 hour.

SHERRIED ORANGE RICE

Ingredients:		METRIC
1/2	cup uncooked long grain white rice	115 g.
1/2	teaspoon salt	2 ml.
1/4	teaspoon thyme	1 ml.
1/8	cup minced onion	20 g.
1/4	cup seedless raisins	40 g.
1/2	medium unpeeled orange, sliced 1/8'' thick and quartered	3 mm.
1/2	can (5 1/4oz.) chicken broth	200 ml.
3	tablespoons orange juice	45 ml.
1/4	cup dry Sherry	60 ml.

Preparation:

In a greased casserole combine rice, seasonings, onions, raisins and orange slices. Bring chicken broth, orange juice and Sherry to a boil in a small sauce pan over medium high heat. Pour the boiling liquid over the rice mixture, stir once, cover and bake in a pre-heated oven at 350°F. for about 45 minutes.

AMARETTO DELIGHT

Ingredients:		METRIC
2	large scoops vanilla ice cream	
4	tablespoons Amaretto liqueur	60 ml.

Preparation:

Place a large scoop of vanilla ice cream in each of two parfait glasses or sherbet glasses and drizzle two tablespoons of Amaretto liqueur over each.

Menu

Sole Elégante

Pineapple Salad

Cauliflower in Parsley Butter

Sauternes Rice

Alpine Green

Sauternes Wine

Sole Elégante

SOLE ELEGANTE

Ingredients:		METRIC
2	(6oz.) sole fillets	170 g.
1/2	(5oz.) can minced clams	140 g.
1/4	cup dry white wine	60 ml.
1/2	lemon, juiced	
1/4	cup chopped mushrooms	60 g.
2	tablespoons chopped onions	20 g.
1/8	teaspoon salt	.5 ml.
1/8	teaspoon pepper	.5 ml.
	SAUCE:	
1/4	cup sour cream	60 ml.
1	egg yolk, beaten	
1/2	lemon, juiced	
1/2	tablespoon butter	8 g.
1	teaspoon cornstarch disolved in	3 g.
	2 tablespoons cold water	30 ml.
2	tablespoons grated parmesan cheese	15 g.

Preparation:

Dry the sole fillets with a paper towel and lay them in a baking dish or casserole. Season the fillets with salt, pepper and lemon juice from 1/2 lemon. Spread minced clams (save the clam juice for later), chopped mushrooms and chopped onions over the fish. Roll up each fillet and secure with toothpicks.

Pour wine and clam juice over the roll-ups, cover and bake in a pre-heated oven at 375°F./190°C. for 25 to 30 minutes or until the fish becomes flaky.

Prepare the sauce in a small sauce pan. Blend butter, lemon juice from 1/2 lemon, and sour cream together. Add the fish juice from the roll-ups and bring to a boil over medium heat. As soon as the sauce begins to boil, remove from heat and add egg yolk and cornstarch. Mix together until it thickens and pour this sauce over the fish. Top with grated cheese and place under broiler about 6"/15 cm. from element for about 2 minutes until cheese browns.